TAKING
CONTROL
OF
YOUR LIFE

TAKING CONTROL OF YOUR LIFE

*The Secrets of Successful
Enterprising Women*

GAIL BLANKE
Vice President, Public Affairs, Avon Products, Inc.

and

KATHLEEN WALAS
National Beauty and Fashion Director, Avon Products, Inc.

MASTERMEDIA LIMITED

NEW YORK

Published by MasterMedia Limited.

MASTERMEDIA and colophon are registered trademarks of MasterMedia Limited.

10   9   8   7   6   5   4   3   2   1

Library of Congress Cataloging-in-Publication Data

Blanke, Gail.
    Taking control of your life: the secrets of successful
enterprising women/Gail Blanke and Kathleen Walas.
        p.   cm.
    ISBN 0-942361-18-0
    1. Women in business. 2. Success in business. 3. Avon Products,
Inc. I. Walas, Kathleen. II. Title.
    HD6053.B52   1990
650.1′082—dc20   90-33685
                                                         CIP

Designed by Stanley S. Drate / Folio Graphics Co., Inc.

Manufactured in the United States of America.

CONTENTS

FOREWORD

This book is about choices. In 1886, when Avon first opened its doors and decided to offer an entrepreneurial selling opportunity to women, there were very few choices.

Now, more than one hundred years later, as we approach a new century, the choices available to women cannot be calculated. They can be homemakers, they can be mothers, they can be career women, they can be entrepreneurs—they can be all those things if they choose, or they can be some of those things.

But whatever they choose, it has to be right for them.

It's been a long journey for women over the past century, and along the way it sometimes seemed that women had lost their right to choose, as if society had said that there was only one right way to do things—whether one was trying to be a homemaker or a superwoman.

As we enter the 1990s, a remarkable thing is happening. Women are choosing their own paths and asserting their own special personalities. Each is saying that there is no one way. I'm going to do what's right for me.

Taking Control of Your Life

We dedicate this book to the more than forty million entrepreneurial women who have sold Avon products since its founding more than a century ago. Through them, we have witnessed firsthand the growth and development of American women as they strive for independence and the right to control their own lives—to be the very best they can be.

JAMES E. PRESTON
Chairman and CEO, Avon Products, Inc.

PROLOGUE

~

Women in the United States have become used to change. During the twentieth century, they have seen their roles as homemaker and mother expand to include new opportunities outside the family. No longer just a companion and helper to her husband, a woman during the century now ending won the right to vote and to voice an opinion.

She also won the right to do things on her own, and not be condemned for it. She discovered the excitement of setting a personal goal and the fun of trying to achieve it. But the nine decades just past are only the beginning. Women are on the brink of explosive success in their struggle for self-fulfillment. The 1990s may very well be the decade that women come thundering into their own.

Avon Products is a company that knows a lot about women. Ever since our founding in 1886, our sales force has been composed primarily of women (500,000 sales representatives today in the United States alone), who have sold primarily to women. We are proud to have been one of the first companies in this country to provide an earning opportunity for women. Today we have more women in management positions than any other *Fortune* 500 company.

But what does this mean to you, the reader, and why did we want to write this book? It's simple. Over the years—more than one hundred years—the people at Avon have developed relationships with millions of women. We think that today we're in touch with your needs, your desires, and, most important, the countless opportunities available to you to make your life better. By setting down some of our thoughts and experiences within the covers of a book, we hope that we might be able to share some of these ideas with you.

Since 1987, Avon Products, in partnership with the United States Small Business Administration, has sponsored what we call the Women of Enterprise Awards. These awards are presented annually to a group of women entrepreneurs who have achieved outstanding business success while overcoming considerable hardship, either economic or personal. We have read hundreds of applications from women entrepreneurs from every part of this country. We know what some of you have endured to control your own lives, to make them more meaningful.

For example, one of our 1987 winners, Marie Jackson-Randolph of Detroit, Michigan, overcame severe financial problems, as well as the personal agony of losing three children in a fire in 1979. Jackson-Randolph reconstructed her life and went on to start the largest chain of black-owned day care centers in the United States. Jackson-Randolph was willing to take a chance on her future. She says, "I was inspired by the motivation of a friend who *dared* me to try to be a businesswoman."

As we mention other Women of Enterprise Awards winners throughout this book, you will see additional firsthand examples of courage, ingenuity, and perseverance, as all these hard-working women struggle toward their vision of success and fulfillment.

The desire to have a more meaningful life, and to remove things from our lives that are nonproductive, is probably universal. But how do you go about obtaining a more beautiful life? We would like to share some of those techniques with you. Certain themes run throughout these pages. These are truths that apply to many women, perhaps to you:

▽ You deserve to have the best life possible. There *are* some difficult situations that cannot be changed, and that we just have to live with—chronic illness, for example. But, for the most part, *you* can decide what your life will be.

▽ You can have a better life that is tailor-made to fit *you*. There are no firm rules for happiness. The advice given in William Shakespeare's *Hamlet*— "This above all: to thine own self be true"—applies to every woman. Only you can decide what you want for yourself.

▽ You can change. You can learn new things, and unlearn bad old habits. You are not doomed to stay in the same old rut, but can take chances and learn by doing. There is not a woman alive who was born knowing how to be successful, and happy. Trial and error is the technique used by just about everyone.

▽ We have been in the beauty business since the last century. We believe in the importance of fitness, grooming, attention to the physical self, to your own special image. Looking good is an important component of feeling good. If you manage to put your best, and most attractive, face forward, you will find new energy, increased self-esteem, and easier relationships with those around you. It is definitely in your power to control the impression you make on others. It's pointless not to make a good one.

We will try to make your options clear in the forthcoming chapters. As we said during the 1989 Women of Enterprise Awards program, "There comes a moment in every woman's life when she feels ready to soar, a turning point when she realizes that her life is hers to control, that whatever she wants is attainable if only she dares to risk." That woman could be you.

1

WOMEN LOOKING TOWARD THE TWENTY-FIRST CENTURY

The start of each new decade usually brings predictions that life is about to change dramatically. This is certainly true of the 1990s, since a new century is not very far down the road. Early reports from those who make a living figuring out what we all think, do, and hope to do indicate that there really is a new feeling in this country, a new sense of purpose.

If change *is* in the air, how can you, an American woman, tap into all the good things that will happen during the years to come? What can you take? And what can you give? What are your choices?

Where We've Come From

Women started this century having very few choices. They could:

   ▽ Be wives and mothers.
   ▽ Remain in their parents' houses if they were not

married. Then they usually ended up taking care of those parents as they aged.

▽ Live with a relative. There were lots of unmarried aunts helping with the housework in their brothers' homes around 1910. Or the farm chores if the family was rural.

▽ Get a suitable job. This was usually domestic work, nursing, or teaching. The movies have shown us both live-in governesses and frontier schoolmarms—these are true images.

By mid-century, life had opened up a lot for women. We had:

▽ Gotten the vote.

▽ Been through two wars. During World War II, women went into offices and factories to take the places of the men who were away in the armed services. When the men returned, the women were expected to lay down their hammers and return to their kitchens, Many did so, but they had seen another way of life.

▽ Achieved a certain amount of independence. Women could live on their own, and engage in many occupations previously reserved for men. They were better educated and participated more in making political decisions and establishing social customs.

During the second half of the twentieth century, women found that they wanted more freedom to control their own lives, and needed to enjoy more of life's experiences. They did something about it.

Where We Are Today—A Progress Report

The way we live as we approach the end of this century seems light-years away from the traditional patterns of even thirty years ago. Who would have predicted the following developments?

▽ The basic family unit of father, mother, and 2.2 children has given way to a whole assortment of combinations. New "families" exist that might include people who are unrelated to each other. As long as they are mutually dependent and supportive, anything goes: single parents with children, senior citizens sharing a house, second marriages with children from both marriages, unmarried couples, divorced single-sex adults who are raising their children together.

▽ Women have entered the workforce in large numbers—these days, more women work than do not, a substantial 56 percent. The Bureau of Labor Statistics predicts that by the year 2000, 85 percent of all women between the ages of twenty and fifty-five will be employed.

▽ Sixty percent of all married mothers of children under six work, a 37 percent increase since 1970.

▽ With so many two-paycheck families, many couples are trying to adjust traditional sex roles. It is no longer unheard-of for fathers to change a diaper, or to cook dinner for the family. Although traditions die hard, there is greater understanding by husbands of the double burden of work and family managed by their wives. And wives, especially now that they're coping with a workday themselves, seem better tuned in to the stress that their husbands undergo.

The American Press Agrees: We've Come a Long Way

Perhaps the job of CEO is not usually awarded to a woman, but, according to the November 1989 *Ladies' Home Journal,* "Despite the barriers they must break down, women *have* made some undeniable gains in the corporate world; they now make up 39 percent of managers, an increase of 34 percent since 1980, and that trend is likely to continue."

A special issue of *Newsweek* (Winter/Spring 1990) points out that employers will simply *have* to pay attention to the needs of their workers—skilled workers will be in demand, and if companies want the very best, they will have to take note of the problems of life outside the office. Says *Newsweek:* "We enter the 21st century with a heightened sensitivity to family issues. Helping parents and children is a bottom-line concern, no longer a matter of debate. Economists say the smaller labor force of the future means that every skilled employee will be an increasingly valuable asset."

Consider education: the cover story in the December 4, 1989, *Time,* entitled "Women Face the '90s," tells us that women made up 20 percent of all college undergraduates during the 1950s—they make up a whopping 54 percent today. In 1960, only 34.8 percent of women were in the workforce—that number has climbed to 57.8 percent. Looking back to 1960, *Time* continues: "The number of female lawyers and judges has climbed from 7,500 to 180,000 today, female doctors from 15,672 to 108,200, and female engineers from 7,404 to 174,000."

With so many more millions of women in the workforce, their presence alone has caused change. Women become expert at their jobs, and they want promotions. If they are getting less money than a man would get, they demand pay parity. And, most important, women want the freedom to do new kinds of work. They want to show their creativity, and they want to be able to compete in their chosen fields—with men *or* other women.

The American woman worker has countless faces. Not all women work for corporate America, or, if they do, have executive jobs. The fading image of the yuppie is only part of the picture of the American woman worker. After all, only a small percentage of women who must work, or who want to work, have advanced degrees. Success does not only go to an M.B.A. from a prestigious business school.

Not all woman workers are young. Some are middle-aged, or quite old, women who perhaps have been working ever since they can remember or who are trying to rejoin the workforce now that the children are grown.

Some women are farmers, foresters, potters, bakers, seamstresses, firefighters. Some work part-time, from their homes. Some are salespeople, who might go from house to house, meeting their customers face to face, or who sell products in their offices. The women of America are bus drivers, taxi drivers, drivers who have horse-drawn cabs in New York City's Central Park, ferry pilots in New England.

You should not pay too much attention to the word "lifestyle." Frequently, the media will seem to praise a particular way of living, and describe it as acceptable, and glamorous, to be desired.

Your way of living is your own—you don't have to be trendy. There is no one right way to think, or right job to do, or right way to live. You are you—unique, with your own life history, family, friends, and hopes for the future. You have to formulate your own goals, special to the way you live your life.

You ought to make it the best life possible, and get started now, because why shouldn't a better life start now? One freedom that you enjoy in this country is the freedom to set your own goals, fulfill them, and remain in control of what happens to you.

Our Most Recent Past

We have just completed a decade that has been called by some the "me" years. It sometimes seemed that everyone was out for number one, without any recognition that we all live in a community that includes more than ourselves. During the 1980s:

▽ Wall Street showed us just how greedy people could be. Making millions on insider trading and stock manipulation, some financiers became so carried away that they even lost their sense of self-preservation and ended up in jail.

▽ Lack of attention to social needs by government

and the private sector led to a visible new underclass in our society—the homeless. This group now includes women and children, and may number in the millions.

▽ Some politicians were unethical. Some lost their jobs and some were indicted.

▽ We saw kinds of crimes that we had not seen before. Drug use spread from the inner city to almost every community. Drug dealing became popular with many, both disadvantaged and not. Death from drug overdose was commonplace in some areas, and shared needle use helped to spread the AIDS plague.

▽ Corporations downsized, or were bought, and people on every economic level were out of work, sometimes for the first time in their lives. It was not always easy to find a new job. Job-seekers settled for what they could get.

▽ As workers were displaced, the American tradition of loyalty to one company for life faded quickly. For many, two-way trust was no longer possible or expected.

▽ Worldwide, badly planned treatment of our environment—whether uncontrolled development, casual waste disposal, industrial pollution, or continued hunting of endangered species—sowed the seeds for serious problems in the future.

The above are just trends, and certainly did not exist in every community, every minute of the 1980s. Yet, they were real problems that affected real people—and they still exist today.

The perception existed during the 1980s that the United States had become a dangerous place. A man's home might be his castle, but the streets weren't safe.

Divorce rates were high, and people could no longer count on the extended family of parents, in-laws, and other relatives for support—with child care, for example. The extended family didn't exist. A Minneapolis woman's parents might live in Florida; her in-laws in Arizona.

Ordinary Americans felt that grace and charm were fast disappearing, that their surroundings were becoming brutalized. Their response was to retreat into the shell of their homes and immediate circle of family and friends.

And the work environment? There was lots happening that affected the man or woman worker of the 1980s. Although life was very precarious for some, and jobs were lost, there were people who made a lot of money. They made it working for corporations that made items like computers, selling cars, running service businesses, being stockbrokers, or opening restaurants.

Those who had money spent it. Savings in the nation's banks nearly evaporated. The word "yuppie" was coined, and symbolized a way of living that was both self-indulgent and workaholic. These were the young, urban professionals, college-educated, who staffed the managerial ranks of our corporations. They wanted expensive *things,* adult toys, really. Status symbols, like the BMW and a country retreat, became the dream of many.

Only a tiny portion of working men and women were actually yuppies, but the press made sure that all of America knew about their "lifestyle." At first, they were made to seem glamorous, to be envied, but as the decade ended, both the yuppies themselves and the millions of other Americans who were reading about them became fed up with the image of endless consumption and the pleasing only of oneself.

Where We're Going

Although there *were* many positive elements in the years just past, in general we cannot look at the decade of the 1980s and see much improvement in ethics and morals, or just good old-fashioned looking out for the other guy. We have not really been our brother's keeper. But early signposts indicate that the 1990s are going to be different.

Each generation seems to go through a period of unselfish caring for others. Some of you were part of the social turmoil of the 1960s and remember how many young people were committed to social change, to making things better for the underdog.

Along with this often goes the desire for a personal life that is fulfilling in many ways, for spiritual as well as creative growth.

When priorities change in a culture, a lot of other things change, too. Traditional roles assigned to women, or to ethnic or racial minorities, may be reassessed. With that rethinking may come new opportunities. If society no longer expects the same things from you, you have the liberty to try unfamiliar paths.

What signs do we see already that the 1990s are going to be a truly new decade, with changes that will make us proud, as well as give us a chance to grow?

▿ The yuppie mentality, so well described in the media during the 1980s, seems altered beyond recognition. The workaholic, ambition-driven couples who gave their children over to the care of others almost as soon as they were born appear transformed.

Among young working couples, there is a new desire to really live their lives. Men want to spend time with their children, and their wives seem less interested in making it to the top of the corporate ladder by the time they're thirty. It looks as if the family may be given another chance.

▿ Some working mothers have decided to give up their jobs for the first few years of their babies' lives—or to try part-time work. It's no longer unthinkable to be "just" a wife and mother.

▿ The fast track no longer seems so attractive. Both men and women are rethinking their work priorities. A study in 1988 by the Maryland Bar Association discovered that one-third of their sample of one thousand lawyers were interested in changing careers. They suffered too much stress and had little time for themselves.

▿ Teachers are in, M.B.A.'s are out. There will be more demand for all kinds of teachers, from kindergarten assistants through Ph.D.'s, during the next decades. We're going to pay more attention to education—and concentrate on the humanities.

▿ Real experience is popular. The couch potatoes who got most of their enjoyment from TV have given way to joggers, and amateur painters, and members of a church chorus. People want to travel, and see the world up close.

▽ Attitudes about gender and traditional roles are changing. There are women at West Point, and in the space shuttle.

▽ Men are changing, too. Although not all wives would agree, a 1989 *New York Times* poll about women's changing lives reported that 61 percent of all wives polled felt that their husbands did their fair share of work in the home.

▽ We're showing more understanding of alternative ways of living. Just a few years ago, divorce was discussed in a whisper. Now we accept second marriages, which frequently include his kids and her kids, single-parent households, and a whole spectrum of other kinds of nontraditional living arrangements without thinking much about it.

▽ Religious groups have more members. Ethical dilemmas are discussed in business schools and corporations. Values are important again.

▽ Activism is back in force. The whale, the eagle, the forests, the rivers, the marshlands, our cities, our farms, our water supply—there is a lot that needs to be saved, and environmental conservation is going to be the hot ticket for the 1990s.

▽ People are volunteering. For a long time, women, especially, felt exploited if they were not paid for any work that they did. But now people are once again staffing the hospitals, literacy programs, animal shelters, meal programs, retirement homes—wherever help is needed.

▽ Real help is being given. In 1989, we all read about David Franklin, a former computer salesman in Maine who had made a lot of money and was willing to share. Franklin gave seed money to worthy applicants to help them start small businesses. Once the money was given, he didn't have much left. Why did he do it? "I have a chance to help people make their life-long dreams come true . . ." he said. "This gives me a great deal of satisfaction."

The "Nurturing Nineties"

During the 1970s and 1980s, women proved that they could be successful in a work environment. But there were problems. Although women made good advances, and showed that they were as competent as the men they worked with, the powers who ran things—mostly men—did not want to *stop* running things. Women were not really members of the club, and were, for the most part, promoted only so far. Some accepted it; some got fed up and left to start their own businesses.

But a new value system is becoming popular as we move into the new decade, and we have a different set of role models. We like down-to-earth women, like Barbara Bush, or smart achievers, like Sandra Day O'Connor. We sympathize with the troubles of Geraldine Ferraro, and thrill to the triumphs of Oprah Winfrey. We like success, and we admire women who overcome adversity to achieve success. The media give us a wide choice of women to admire: there's Mother Teresa, and poet and author Maya Angelou, activist actresses like Morgan Fairchild and Joanne Woodward, and all the women who run day care centers in inner cities, and those who are firefighters, and police officers, and try to keep the family farms going. Most visibly, there are millions of women entrepreneurs, more, in fact, than at any other time in our history.

THE AGE OF THE WOMEN ENTREPRENEURS

Women entrepreneurs take a chance on themselves. They sell encyclopedias, buy franchises, become consultants, start dog-walking services, or open hair-styling salons. They do it on their own, or with partners, but they are working for *themselves* to gain control over their own personal and financial destinies. According to the United States Small Business Administration:

> ▽ The woman business owner now makes up the fastest-growing sector of the small business community. At present, they own 30 percent of the nation's businesses.
> ▽ Between 1980 and 1986, the number of businesses owned by women increased by 64 percent, from 2.5 million to 4.1 million.
> ▽ Businesses owned by men increased by only 33 percent.
> ▽ In 1980, women-owned businesses generated $36 billion. That figure climbed to $72 billion in 1986, an increase of 100 percent.

19 ❧

WOMEN'S ABILITIES

Women have become visible and powerful enough to have a voice in how we live our lives. And if we really are entering an era of caring, and involvement, who better than women to lead the way?

Women have special concerns and abilities that many men do not have. For example:

▽ Creativity. They can figure out new ideas for new situations. They're not bound by foggy tradition.

▽ Common sense (sometimes called "street smarts").

▽ A well-developed system of values. Women know what's important. They know how to get support from their families when they need it. And they value friendship, and loyalty.

▽ Enthusiasm and dedication. They inspire others to work with them.

▽ Patience. They will see a job through.

▽ Affection. Women are not detached, not cold. In a work situation, most women will involve the whole team and be personally and enthusiastically involved with the job and the personnel.

▽ Intuition. Yes, women's intuition does exist. And it can be a vital ingredient in making a decision.

▽ A desire to be happy. Most women are not interested in doing in the competition. They want good teamwork and a pleasant work environment.

▽ The ability to listen. This is invaluable both at work and at home. It is the basis for communication. And many important things in life are based on the understanding good communication brings.

The above are the skills for the nineties. They will be needed in every area of our lives—business, personal, political, artistic. Women possess these traits. They will have the opportunity to show us all how society can be improved with the application of understanding and common sense. Women will care about doing an excellent job, and they will care about contented workers. Why shouldn't our lives be easier? And why shouldn't we all feel more connected to each other? If women are given the chance, they will show American society how our lives can be made more beautiful.

2

AM I ALL I CAN BE?

"**I**t takes as much energy to be miserable as it does to be happy," says Dr. Deborah Bright, motivational consultant. "So you might as well live your life positively and energetically."

Dr. Bright is 100 percent correct. This is your life. It's all you're ever going to have. If you don't make it the best it can possibly be, you will be wasting a precious opportunity. And what about your friends, your family, your co-workers, all of those lives that touch yours?

Every Christmas season, we see on TV one of the best inspirational movies ever made: *It's a Wonderful Life*. In this 1946 film, James Stewart, playing a small-town banker, comes upon hard times. In despair, he wonders if those he loves wouldn't be better off if he were dead. He thinks about suicide. But this is a Hollywood fantasy, and an angel intervenes. The angel shows our hero what effect his life has had on those around him, and what would have happened if he had never lived. He sees the good that he has done others in his lifetime, and how he has been part of a helping, caring community.

The viewer also learns the lesson: we each influence others in thousands of ways. Not everything that we do is beneficial, but there are those who depend on us, and who care about us. It is also a basic psychological truth that we feel good about ourselves when we concentrate on helping our friends and family. It's a win-win situation. We give needed help, and feel good about it. And we've done something useful for someone else. When it's our turn to need something, presumably we will be repaid in kind. It also may be true that taking care of each other is the only way that life on this planet can get better.

Control Your Life—It's Basic

How do we achieve that "best that we can possibly be"? And what is it, realistically? As we review the life experiences of the thousands of women that we've worked with, it seems clear that the "best" is different for each woman. There is, however, one theme that exists in every story of a woman overcoming hardship to achieve her dream of success. We hear again and again of the necessity for each woman to have as much control as possible over her life: to stand on her own two feet. A life *out* of control lacks direction and satisfaction. And a life without direction, without goals, is a life that is flat and uninteresting.

It is human nature to want to know where we're going. We need to plan our futures, to work toward concrete goals for ourselves and our families. The women of America have been working hard to make life better for themselves and their families since the days of the pioneers in this country. There have always, of course, been the privileged few. But the majority of women through the years have had to figure out the best way to support themselves and their families, economically and emotionally, since settlements began. There were probably enterprising women in the days of the Stone Age who put aside a few perfect flint arrowheads to trade for some fur wraps to keep their children alive during the bitter winter. Women have always struggled, and those who persevered succeeded.

Our Women of Enterprise Awards winners know this. Carolyn A. Stradley, a 1989 winner, overcame almost insurmountable odds to found C&S Paving, a general contracting company in Georgia whose annual billings currently exceed $2.5 million. But the road that Stradley traveled to reach this plateau was winding and difficult—so difficult that the listener hears her story with awe and admiration.

Stradley was born to poverty in an Appalachian mountain community, child of an alcoholic father and a chronically ill mother. "Some of my earliest memories are of my father being drunk and breaking things," she recalls.

When Carolyn Stradley was only eleven, her mother died. She and her older brother found themselves in effect orphaned, as their father disappeared and left the children to fend for themselves. They struggled to survive the cold winter. There was no money, so food was largely wild berries, bitter pokeweed salad, and the occasional stew cooked up from rabbits they caught themselves. At school—grammar school—Stradley washed dishes and swept floors to earn the lunch that she could not pay for.

Stradley's brother moved to Atlanta in an attempt to find a better life, and after her thirteenth birthday Stradley followed him. She managed to attend high school, supporting herself by waitressing at night.

Life improved for Stradley when she was fifteen: she fell in love with twenty-six-year-old Arthur Stradley, who was employed as a machine operator, and the couple married while Stradley was still in high school. Unfortunately, when the school learned that she was pregnant, she was expelled.

But the Stradleys were doing fine. Carolyn worked as a secretary for a local construction company, learning the business, and the couple enjoyed their middle-class existence. They were employed, they had a house, two cars, and by now their baby daughter had been born.

Came 1969—and disaster. Arthur Stradley contracted a strep infection that settled in his kidneys. First he became very ill, then totally disabled. And, once again, Carolyn Stradley had to focus all her inner resources on surviving. For the next four years, she managed a routine of full-time job, motherhood, evening classes, and caring for her husband: twice a week she monitored Arthur's all-night kidney treatment on the dialysis machine.

Arthur Stradley's health did not improve, and once again—in 1973—Carolyn was left on her own when Arthur died of a heart attack. Stradley remembers her fear: "I was afraid I'd be cold and alone again." But she persevered. Her daughter needed her, and she did not give up her studies in construction engineering at Georgia Tech. She still looked to the future.

Only a year after Arthur's death, Carolyn Stradley began to move up the ladder at her company—she was promoted to division manager.

After two more years of construction experience, Stradley thought that it was time for real independence, the adventure of being her own boss. But the local banks were not impressed by her excellent credit rating—construction and asphalt paving did not seem to be a suitable business for a woman.

Stradley was not about to quit. Her brother and sister-in-law came to help, and they set up the business at Stradley's kitchen table. She was on her way.

C&S Paving took on any job—the small jobs that no one else wanted—and they kept going, step by step. Stradley frequently worked fifteen-hour days, sometimes running the heavy machinery herself. The profits were reinvested in the business, and slowly the company gained financial success. Carolyn Stradley found personal happiness again with Leon Thompson, also a general contractor, whom she married in 1984. C&S Paving continued to prosper, and in 1985 the firm was awarded the contract for a project at Dobbins Air Force Base—an especially sweet assignment because it was the largest United States Air Force contract ever awarded a woman-owned business.

Carolyn Stradley is an inspirational example of the value of perseverance—she succeeded because she never gave up. Today, she gives back to society from her success. Always remembering those grindingly difficult early years, she works with abused children, with women in Georgia's prisons, with parolees and exchange students. Stradley is an admired role model in her community.

She does have some advice for women who are trying to make a place for themselves in *their* world. Says Stradley: "First, set a goal. Know what it is you want or where you are going with your life—take control. Second, educate yourself for that goal using perseverance and creativity. Third, I rely on Divine Guidance. Realize that the peace of mind inside you is worth more than any bank account."

Your Dreams Can Be Your Reality

We see from the above story how Carolyn Stradley has managed her life. She turns to her faith for inner peace—it's very important to have a philosophy, or a religion, or a pattern of beliefs, to help you emotionally through the hard times. And the rest of Stradley's advice is practical: know what you want, set a goal, and then start achieving it step by step. Educate yourself. Make sure that you know what you need to know. Do things look bleak? They certainly did to Carolyn Stradley. Her early life was littered with setbacks. But she chose to concentrate her energies on positive thinking, not despair, and she never gave up.

WHY IS HAVING CONTROL OVER YOUR LIFE IMPORTANT?

In its definition of "control," *The Random House Dictionary* talks about dominating, or commanding. *Webster's* is gentler, and mentions guiding, and managing. But however you see control, it is what puts you in charge of your *own* life, and makes you responsible for what happens to you. Then you have no excuses. If you're happy, congratulations, you did a fine job. If not, it's never too late to try to make things better.

Children have hardly any control over their own lives. But the nice thing about growing up is that life's choices are then yours. Gaining control gives you the power:

1. To define yourself in other people's eyes. You can control what people think of you. Obviously, good human relationships make for a happier life.

2. To refuse to be a victim. No one can bully you. You can say, "Stop. I won't permit this behavior. I don't like it."

3. To help others. If your life is in order, you can help your family and friends emotionally. If your work life is in order, you can help them financially.

4. To choose. You can decide what you want to do. Do you want to work? Get married? Move? Whatever is best for you.

5. To change. If you are in control, you see that it's possible to do something else, or be a different way.

6. To develop more confidence. If you see yourself as being in control, you're bound to feel more confident with every new success.

7. To be free. Control of your life is the only way that you won't feel trapped, whether it's in a bad relationship or a bad job. You will have the courage to get out.

8. To fulfill your dreams. Control gives you a

sense that you can manage your own future. If you are confident, you will take risks. If you take risks, you have the possibility of greater rewards.

WORKING THROUGH PROBLEMS

It is possible to work through problems and construct the sort of life that is satisfying, stimulating, and financially rewarding. Do you want that kind of life? Probably everyone wants, needs, and deserves the best life possible for them. One that is beautiful in their own terms.

Do you have fantasies of what life could be like for you? Do you make lists of all the things you would do if you suddenly found a trunk of pirate's gold at the beach? We all have these dreams. But in real life we rarely stumble across the pot of gold at the end of the rainbow.

But that doesn't matter. Most dreams are realistic dreams, and they don't always involve great riches. You might wish for good health for your children, a more fulfilling way for your husband to make a living, or for a better job for yourself. Perhaps you want improved relationships with your in-laws, or you might wish you *had* in-laws, and the husband to go with them.

Carolyn Stradley had to overcome a great deal. There are hundreds of other women like her. Women who have decided that they indeed do want a better life, that they don't want to wait for it forever, and that it is within their power to get it for themselves. They know that they can control their own destinies, and many of them are working toward their individual goals right now.

The sense of women being able to control their lives is in the air in this country. We see articles in popular magazines, we see women on TV telling about their successes gained after overcoming serious adversity. There is a popular song written by Annie Lennox and Dave Stewart of the rock group Eurythmics called "Sisters Are Doin' It for Themselves." The lyric describes how at one time women relied only on men, but now they're coming out of the kitchen and becoming doctors, lawyers, politicians—they're standing on their "own two feet." They're helping other women, and they're succeeding on their own, relying on themselves.

Talk shows are popular because we all want to hear how people—rich and famous or average folks—manage to get their lives in order. Oprah Winfrey is very much admired because of what she has achieved—coming up from nothing. Her success is due to her own drive, and the result seems to be not only fabulous economic resources—and the power to do just as she pleases in the entertainment business, complete control of what she does for a living—but true contentment with her lot in life. And she keeps trying to get *everything* she wants. The nation lived through her diet, and applauded the new look that she obviously yearned for. Why shouldn't she be successful? Oprah Winfrey is willing to work for it. And she continues to dream.

The women whom we have met across the country are, for the most part, ordinary women. They are not likely to sell gold records or be on the cover of *Time* magazine or be familiar names in households in Scandinavia. The content of a life can often be satisfying if the person living that life wants it to be so. Great fame, wealth, international recognition do not seem to have the power to confer happiness or satisfaction. We have only to look to a few of our American household names who lived much of their lives in misery and eventually lost control of those lives. The list is very long, but we can start by thinking of Marilyn Monroe, Judy Garland, Janis Joplin—stars who had everything going for them, but they had no inner peace.

You deserve to have a beautiful life, and in order to do that, you must have good control over the elements of your life. Not everything is within your control, and not everything that is less than perfect in your life *can* be changed. Everyone has some constraints that affect life fundamentally. It may be that:

∇ You or a member of your family has a chronic health problem, or a disability of some sort. Maybe you must live near a certain hospital or in a warm climate.

∇ You have care-taking responsibilities for now. Perhaps you oversee one child, or several children, or an aged relative or in-law. These are usually constraints that change eventually.

∇ You hate what you're doing, but you do it well and make a good salary, and your family is dependent on you financially.

∇ Your racial or ethnic background prevents you from succeeding in certain ways. You may be living in a part of this country that harbors certain traditional prejudices against people of your background. You love your house, which your grandparents built, you feel comfortable in your community, and you don't want to leave. Getting a better life for yourself would involve some tough decisions, maybe moving to a different area.

There are, of course, many other examples of situations in life over which you have no control, or very little. There is really only one answer for you, and it's found in the words of the American theologian Reinhold Niebuhr: you "change what you can, accept what you cannot change, and ask for the wisdom to know the difference."

"The Only Thing You Have to Fear Is Fear Itself"?

You may think that trying to gain control over your life is all very interesting . . . for other readers. You may see the way that you live as being quite okay for you, with nothing in it too terrible, no important dreams unfulfilled—at least none that are possible—and, besides, you're probably too old to change.

But that sort of thinking ought to be unacceptable. Never compare yourself to others—you cannot possibly know what kind of life someone else is living unless you are actually that person. You can, however, figure out what kind of life that *you're* living. Once women decide what they really want in their lives, nothing can stop them except a lack of confidence. It is that basic fear of failure that prevents the first step. Fear *can* be overcome. When it *is* overcome, confidence is born. Then anything is possible.

35

By 1960, Eleanor Roosevelt, partner and wife of President Franklin Delano Roosevelt—who in 1933 had told a desperate nation that "The only thing we have to fear is fear itself"—had become a vibrant force for social good throughout the world. She said in that year, "You gain strength, courage, and confidence by every experience in which you really stop to look fear in the face."

Eleanor Roosevelt understood fear. Although she was born to great wealth and privilege, she was a shy young girl who often felt out of place among her prominent friends and relatives. When she married her handsome cousin Franklin, she embarked on a life in the public eye, and was forced to overcome what was one of the most awkward social presences of this century.

Mrs. Roosevelt was not a glamorous woman physically, and throughout adulthood retained much of her painful girlhood shyness. In addition, she was burdened with a rather scratchy, high voice, which, coupled with the upper-class accent of her background, sometimes made her hard to understand.

But Eleanor Roosevelt persevered. She was dedicated to her many causes, and wanted to get her points across as clearly as possible, on the radio and at organizational meetings ranging from a local chamber of commerce to the United Nations. She took public speaking instruction, and learned to modulate her voice. Because the people that she was trying to help were more important to her than her own self-consciousness, she forced herself to ignore her shyness. Little by little, she became one of the most inspirational, dedicated speakers in the post–World War II world, and was instrumental in many positive social changes.

That was then. What about now? Have women of our time made a decision to work toward their cherished goals? It does seem as though women are tired of taking a backseat in their personal and business lives. Many women feel that their lives are not as rich and rewarding as they deserve, and they want more. They want better lives for themselves, and their families, and for other women as well.

But in order to achieve that, women must continue to amass financial, and political, clout. They must continue to contribute to the economic life of this country, and they must make their wishes clear in the voting booth. No one will give us anything. We must earn it for ourselves.

If we can manage it, it will only benefit the country. Women, with their different approach to governing, and living, with their nurturing abilities, can make this country a more pleasant place to live and work. They can become a force for good. Women can do anything if they first help themselves. Helping others will follow.

Where Do You Stand?

Are you one of those women who, when asked by someone who really wants to know, "How are you doing?" will answer, "Just fine" or "Really excellent" or "I'm cool" or "Thank y'all for askin'. I'm real good," depending on your age and the part of the country that you call home? Why don't you really think about those answers? It may be that your life is as satisfying as you can make it. That it's just right for you. You may have good friends, a loving family, self-satisfaction through paid employment or volunteer work. You may ask for nothing more.

But while such situations do exist, most women, if they were to think about it, would discover that there are things about their lives that they would like to change—and would also discover that many of the things that they would like to change might even be changeable.

For example, you might like to:

∇ Earn more money.
∇ Learn new ways of doing things. Investigate a new field.
∇ Become a force for good. Help people. Help other women get ahead.
∇ Show how courageous you can be. Take risks. Remember the Cowardly Lion in the Oz books? He was brave all along. He just didn't realize it. You're probably in the same boat.
∇ Show a little creativity. You have a lot of ideas, but you've never had a chance to try them out.
∇ Be independent. You're tired of working nine to five. You don't have any time to spend with your children.
∇ Define your own job. Work out your own schedule.

If any of these goals seem attractive to you, they are well within your grasp—with just a little planning.

The chapters in this book concentrate on the "you" that gets out in the world, meets people, tries to start a business or develop a career. There will be no guidance concerning the personal areas of your life—your relationships with your husband, parents, children, or the possible emotional damage you might have suffered because of problems in your life. If you find that most areas of your life are truly gray, that you live with misery every day and see no way out, please seek professional help.

But if you feel more or less in control, spend a few minutes thinking about your life as it appears to you. Think about the whole you: the way you see your life, with its responsibilities to others and to yourself, and also the physical you on which so much depends. You need a healthy body to actually do the things you want to do—it should be in optimum condition, the best you can make it. And you want that physical self to look as good as it can—the better you look, the better the reaction you will get from others, and the easier you will find your human relationships.

Read through the checklist below, and answer either yes or no. Sometimes a "yes" is worth one point, sometimes a "no." But if you finish up with more than five points, it might be time for you to think carefully about how you spend your days, and about the structure of your life. And it is definitely time for you to read through the remaining chapters in this book.

Am I in Control of My Life?

1. Think back to when you were in high school. Have your adolescent dreams been fulfilled, at least the ones that were realistic?

Yes _____ No _____

2. Have you had to compromise a lot over the years because people who were important to you— your parents, spouse—had different expectations of you?

Yes _____ No _____

3. Now that you're more or less past adolescence, do you still have dreams? Not about winning the lottery. Dreams that can be fulfilled—like taking college-level courses.

Yes _____ No _____

4. How busy are you? Do you find that there are never enough hours in the day?

Yes _____ No _____

5. Are the things that keep you busy (if you are busy) pretty much the same day after day, season after season?

Yes _____ No _____

6. How do you feel when you wake up in the morning? With a song in your heart, or is it more likely to be bored resignation?

Yes, I'm bored _____   No, life is a joy _____

7. Your children are always learning something new. How about you? Do you have frequent new experiences, whether you're employed or not?

Yes _____   No _____

8. Do you have good times with your family? Do you go on trips? Play new games together? Enjoy group projects?

Yes _____   No _____

9. If you have a family, do you find that you usually have something of interest to say to them?

Yes _____   No, they seem to find me dull _____

10. If you do not work, do you feel guilty about not making a contribution to the family funds?

Yes _____   No _____

11. If you do work, do you like your job? Are you enthusiastic about it?

Yes _____   No _____

12. Look at yourself in a full-length mirror. Do you like what you see?

Yes, I look great _____ No _____

13. Have there been significant changes in your appearance in the last five years? Have you gained or lost a lot of weight, for example?

Yes _____ No _____

14. Have you neglected your health? Forgotten about checkups? Gynecologist? Mammography? Dentist?

Yes _____ No _____

15. Do you have three different wardrobes? Depending on whether your latest diet was successful?

Yes _____ No _____

16. Take a hard look at your wardrobe. Do you have items you haven't worn during the year?

Yes _____ No _____

17. Is your wardrobe dated? Not suitable to the way you live now?

Yes _____ No _____

18. Do you have clothes for any occasion that

might come up? Sportswear, business clothes, at least one dressy outfit?

Yes _____ No _____

19. How about accessories? Shoes in the right colors? Scarves to match your various outfits? Gloves, and hats if you wear them? In other words, can you get it together in a matter of minutes?

Yes _____ No _____

20. What about your makeup? Still using that old mascara from two years ago? And Aunt Katherine's lipstick that she left in your apartment?

Yes _____ No _____

Give yourself one point for each matching answer:

1.	No	11.	No
2.	Yes	12.	No
3.	No	13.	Yes
4.	No	14.	Yes
5.	Yes	15.	Yes
6.	Yes	16.	Yes
7.	No	17.	Yes
8.	No	18.	No
9.	No	19.	No
10.	Yes	20.	Yes

Add up your points. The lower the number, the more in control of your life you are.

0–5   You're very much in control and need just minor adjustments.

6–12   You're somewhat in control. Check through the statements to find areas that need adjusting. Pick one to start working on immediately.

13–20   If you are in this range, you might ask yourself these questions: Have I become stagnant? Have my dreams and goals—sometimes quite simple goals—been put on the back burner for no really good reason? What do I really want?

Don't let lethargy be an enemy. Whatever you want you can probably have. You can learn to think positively. Believe in all the others who have gone before you. In the words of Marie Jackson-Randolph, one of our 1987 Women of Enterprise, "Success is the realization that you are capable of anything if you have the requisite mindset." So please think about it. You *can* find the energy to take that first step. Others have. You can, too.

3

THE TURNING POINT

Rags-to-Riches: The American Dream

Have you ever heard of Horatio Alger? Sure you have, in passing. But if you'd lived at the end of the last century, you might actually have read the stories by the Reverend Mr. Alger. These best-selling tales usually tell of a poor child who, through pluck, ingenuity, and good luck, climbs the ladder of success. The hero always succeeds with the help of a wiser and richer being who recognizes the central character's good qualities.

These basic themes are still alive and well today. In fact, they're fundamental to the traditional rags-to-riches idea of American success. We can all relate to these ideas. We are, after all, a nation of immigrants. Most of us are descended from recent generations who either traveled here from distant countries to find a better life—or were forced to come in the holds of the slave ships. Most of us are born into families that want always to improve—each generation should live better, know more, be happier, than the one that came before.

"We Have Had Enough"

This dream has come true for some. It has not come true for everyone. We know that there are things in our lives that we cannot change. But there are things that we *can* change. There are women all across the country who are finally saying, "We have had enough." These are women who know that they can make a better life for themselves and their families, and who are beginning to understand that there are opportunities available to them.

Some women are tired of:

▽ Having to be superwomen. Juggling work, family, and community life can extract an enormous toll.

▽ Having to function as second-class citizens in the business world. Men still receive most of the larger salaries, and the top jobs. Frequently, it's unusual for women to be taken seriously. It's hard, for example, to get bank loans to start up a new business, even if the applicant is demonstrably competent and a good risk.

▽ Hearing that a woman's place is in the home. Although some men are more sensitive to the needs of women than they used to be, women still are expected to do the bulk of parenting and housework, even if they are in the workforce as well.

As we enter the last decade of this century, it appears that the women of America may have a chance to lead the way in trying to find a more meaningful, rewarding life. They're the ones who have the most to gain—and nothing to lose. The economic powers in this country are not going to march up to each woman's front door and say, "Please, we have a more interesting life out here for you. Won't you give it a try?" It's up to each woman to find that more interesting life for herself.

Are you a woman who is ready to see what's out there? You may have learned in chapter 1 that your life has been on hold for years. To take the next step, all you need are:

▽ The knowledge that things can be better. That your life, although it may be reasonably okay, can be better for you.

▽ A sense of excitement. THIS IS *YOUR* LIFE. It is the only one that you will ever have. Do you really want to reach the end of your life and know that you didn't pull out all the stops and go for it? That's why you were put on this earth. To make the most of yourself, to live life to the fullest.

▽ The realization that your dreams are as worthwhile as anyone else's. And you deserve the good things in life as much as anyone else. No one has the right to say, "This person deserves to be happy. That person does not."

▽ Energy. Get your mind working if it hasn't been for some time. You're smart. Don't let your life get away from you because you are too lethargic to make sensible plans.

▽ Curiosity. Aren't you curious to see what could

happen in your life if you really tried? If you do what you've always done in your life, you'll get what you've always gotten. What might happen if you tried something else?

▽ Creativity. Haven't you always suspected that you could sell those beautiful handmade sweaters that you've been giving away for years? The ones that your grandchildren think are great? All you have to do to start is to pack up a few of them and visit the owner of the boutique on the next block. Maybe you'll make a sale. It's a waste of your life's energy just to wonder—you could be converting your dreams into action.

▽ Confidence. It's not too constructive for you to be told that all you need is confidence when you find it difficult to address a group larger than your immediate family. But do not despair—most people feel that way. Memoirs of famous people are full of the techniques they've tried to overcome attacks of insecurity: they range from hypnotism to imagining that everyone in the audience is naked.

▽ Self-esteem. This is, of course, that part of confidence you feel deep inside. The little voice that tells you that you are as good, as capable, as intelligent, as important as anyone else on earth. You are all of those things.

A Matter of Choice

We have all heard women, again and again, in describing how they live, talk as if they have no control over their own lives, no choice in what becomes of them. Why do they think that? Do you fall into that category? And if you do, why do you?

Most of you are in a living arrangement that is more or less flexible, where you are engaged in situations in which you have an adult voice in making decisions. There are those few of you who are enmeshed in a problematical relationship: an abusive spouse, difficult children, parents who are ill. These may be situations for which you need professional counseling.

But for most of you, any lethargy, stagnating, lack of drive, acceptance of the status quo, comes mainly from within yourself—these are not externally driven situations or feelings. There are opportunities out there that are just right for you. What are the feelings that are holding you back?

It seems clear that self-esteem lies at the bottom of all dreams and possibilities. This is true no matter what your line of work. You may be a computer programmer, a short-order cook, deep-sea diver, or very famous person. Dolly Parton has said, "I've got more confidence than I do talent, I think. Confidence is the main achiever of success."

Most people don't realize that they *can* change. That it's actually within their own power. And that they don't need anyone's permission. What all women should try to remember when contemplating any sort of change is that very little is carved in granite—in most areas of your life you can erase, edit, rewrite. And the operative word is *you*—you are the actor, and you and yours reap the benefits. You just have to have the confidence to know that you'll succeed.

Confidence can be developed. Self-esteem is something that we grow into. Almost no one is born with either one. You learn step by step, through small successes. Small successes build upon each other, and turn into large successes. Failure is a habit. So is success. You get used to one or the other, so you might as well get used to success.

You need to think about:

▽ Your self-knowledge. Are you confident that you have a clear understanding of what your life is like? Do you know if you're happy?
▽ Your purpose in life. You don't want to drift forever. Do you know what your main goals are?
▽ What opportunities you can take advantage of. There are all kinds of brass rings to grab at. You have to figure out which ones you want.

Into Each Life a Lot of Rain Can Fall

True heroism is very often the triumph of an ordinary woman who finds herself in an extraordinary situation. That situation may revolve around a financial setback, or emotional upheaval due to death or divorce or, as in the case of Sydney A. Stoeppelwerth, a serious physical challenge.

Sydney Stoeppelwerth, now fifty-two, is one of our 1988 Women of Enterprise, and a paragon of self-reliance. The decade of the nineties may prove to be a time when women all over the country are going to stand up and say, "We know that we can take care of ourselves. And we will prove it by taking control of our *own* lives."

Stoeppelwerth believes in self-reliance and says, "I am responsible for what happens to me. To demand from others before one demands of oneself negates progress. You must have a positive attitude." This is an admirable belief from any woman trying to make her way, but what makes it quite astonishing in this case is that Sydney Stoeppelwerth has been totally blind since the age of twenty-seven.

Today Stoeppelwerth enjoys a successful, multifaceted career as a motivational speaker, entrepreneur, and counselor, but her climb has been long and difficult. She credits her positive attitude with helping her over the rough spots: "One need not see to see," says Stoeppelwerth. "Everyone has a physical inconvenience sometimes. Some are just more obvious than others." With such an accepting, yet proactive approach to life's insecurities, it is easy to see why Stoeppelwerth, in her lectures and workshops, has inspired thousands of listeners to achieve personal and professional growth.

Sydney Stoeppelwerth had always planned on becoming a teacher, but when she was nineteen she learned that she would someday become blind. Planning for a challenged future, she completed her degree in English from the University of Kansas. After losing her sight, Stoeppelwerth continued teaching, but for eight years went no further than tutoring students at home. But basic to her personality is the desire, as she says today, for "new challenge, new opportunities, growth, and expansion." The need for new frontiers is bolstered by her solid support system of values: "self-reliance, honesty, integrity, persever-ance, persistence, and conviction."

It is no wonder that she wanted broader horizons than those offered by tutoring: Stoeppelwerth wanted nothing less than a job teaching in the public school system. She applied to the master's program at the University of Missouri, but was turned down. Certain that it was because her blindness seemed to others to be insurmountable, she convinced the dean to accept her for a probationary period: then they could evaluate her chances for success. After a semester of straight A's, she became a fully matriculated student.

Eventually, success rewarded Stoeppelwerth's ef-forts and she became the only blind teacher ever hired in the Shawnee Mission School District in Johnson County, Kansas.

New challenges followed successes to be followed by new challenges. In a search for greater financial rewards than were available to her as a schoolteacher, Stoeppelwerth embarked on a series of varied entre-preneurial enterprises: first oil production ("Since no one can see underground, I knew I had a fair chance to compete in the oil business simply by using my head") and then a motivational speaking company.

Stoeppelwerth travels, drives a boat, water skis, knits, and is active in local educational and arts organ-izations. "I'm going to play tennis when I find some-one who manufactures tennis balls with buzzers in them," she says. A full life, indeed. Sydney Stoeppel-werth is too busy thinking about the next thing that she's going to conquer to worry about problems of confidence. She *knows* she can do it.

A phrase that we hear frequently from the Women

of Enterprise winners is "If I can do it, anyone can." They usually go on to mention that they are just ordinary women, from ordinary backgrounds, with ordinary abilities. Yet they are often women who have overcome a great deal in their lives without falling to pieces—and if they did at one time stumble, then they have managed to pick themselves up again, usually with some humor, and gone on to personal successes of various sorts.

Judith Briles, D.B.A., a specialist in women's issues, is now a speaker, author (of *The Confidence Factor,* among other books), and management consultant. In advising others, Dr. Briles often can relate to their problems in overcoming emotional and physical pain, as she herself has survived the death of two children, multiple business reversals, and a terrifying bout with IUD-caused paralysis that lasted for several months. She is a fervent believer in the power of positive thinking—in each life, there is always something to be grateful for.

"No matter what has happened to you—whatever tragedy you've had to live through, business troubles, bad health—no matter how bad it is, there are always people far worse off than you are," says Dr. Briles. Some years ago, she had a breast cancer scare, and while she waited for what ultimately turned out to be good news, she accepted the worst, and thought: "Well, if it's bad news, I know that there are worse things. After all, I'd rather lose a breast than a hand," she said to herself, "or a foot."

Judith Briles believes that visualization is a useful technique in overcoming any kind of pain, in regaining confidence. "When times are rough," she advises, "start imagining yourself leading a happy life. Try to stop thinking negatively. See the good in your life. Get rid of negative influences, including those friends and relatives who are dragging you down. Ask yourself where you're going from here. Try to imagine what you'd like to be doing this time next year. You can make it happen."

Dr. Briles points out that we all have choices. You can stay stuck in whatever situation you find yourself in, trusting to luck to get you out, or you can try to get out yourself. The choice is yours to make—it's not given to you by your husband, your children, your parents, your business associates, your friends. You yourself can choose to live life to the fullest.

Are You Afraid of Success?

It may be that you're actually afraid of success. When we talk about "success," we don't necessarily mean just monetary success. We're referring to a successful *life,* which may or may not include being especially well off financially. We mean a successful life for *you,* one that fulfills your heart's desire, a life in which you are the best that you can possibly be.

But whatever kind of success we mean, you may not be ready for it. Although we may be entering in this country a time that will see the empowerment of women, one that will be accepting of their influence, their nurturing abilities, and their compassion, women in the United States have not been expected up to now to be leaders, or trend-setters, or agents for change.

There have, of course, always been exceptions,

and we've seen countless influential women in various fields who have wielded as much power as comparable men. But at the grass-roots level of American culture, even as we approach the end of the century, there is still a powerful theme that says that women are the "little women," whose job it is to tend the hearth, and raise the children, and work only out of direst financial necessity. Men are the breadwinners, continues this idea, and even if their wives *are* working, they still rule the roost in their own homes.

"Women today sometimes are faced with a double standard," says New York City–based psychotherapist Natalia Zunino, Ph.D. "On the one hand, they sometimes *have* to get out into the workplace, or they want to, but how are they supposed to act when they get there? Like men? What will the men think? And what about their femininity?" Dr. Zunino points out that there are still serious problems of role expectation in our culture, as well as stereotypes that are sometimes hard to overcome.

"Women are often brought up to believe that they have made a contract with society that forces them to behave in a certain way. Then, if you act in a way that is not expected by society—if you behave forcefully on the job, for example—then some women might feel guilty, as if they're changing the rules once the game has begun.

"Of course," continues Dr. Zunino, "the wonderful thing about breaking such a contract is that some women discover talents that they never knew they had. Because conformity, and not experimentation, is rewarded in many families, especially if the children are female, if women do, as adults, try new things, they may discover abilities that they never dreamed of when they were young. And with these new talents comes renewed self-esteem."

Along with renewed confidence comes the elimination of the fear of trying something new. This is altogether a winning situation.

How do you see your proper place in society? Answer the questions in the following quiz and see if you are afraid of success, of standing out in any way.

How to Determine If You Fear Success

Answer yes or no to the following.

1. If you are a working parent, do you still see child care and housework as being mostly your responsibility?

2. When you and your husband talk about your jobs, do you do most of the listening?

3. Is your job the best you can get? Does it give you what you want out of life?

4. Are you taking training or courses to move you up the ladder a step?

5. You have what you think is a good, simple idea for a small business. You also know people in your family or community who could help you develop the idea. Are you hesitant to ask for assistance?

6. You think you'd like to go back to school to finish your B.A., but you know that means putting your own needs first. Does that bother you?

7. If you do land a very good job, and are success-

ful at it, do you think your friends and family are going to resent you?

8. You work, but your salary is small and you're unhappy about it. Do you take steps to earn more?

9. Do you find that you defer to your husband when making important decisions that affect your life together?

10. You've chosen to be a full-time homemaker. Do you spend most of your day watching television, and wishing you were more active in your community?

Compare your answers with the following:

	Ready for Success	*Afraid of Success*
1.	No	Yes
2.	No	Yes
3.	Yes	No
4.	Yes	No
5.	No	Yes
6.	No	Yes
7.	No	Yes
8.	Yes	No
9.	No	Yes
10.	No	Yes

You can tell at a glance whether you are too retiring to aim high. If you really want something different, you might try changing some yeses to noes and vice versa.

A Matter of Control

Why do you want greater control over your life? After all, things have been going along reasonably well up to now. But you will never know until you try how much better you *could* feel about your life—about your family, and spouse, and the opportunities open to you. Control means having the confidence to change your life if you want to—to decide to do something, to plan a desired result, and then have the discipline and know-how to follow through.

What are some of the benefits of greater control? They would, of course, differ for each woman, but at the very least greater control can help you to:

▽ Eliminate some of the overwhelming uncertainties in life. Life can be full of unpleasant surprises. But if you have goals, and have figured out, even theoretically, a way to reach them, then your existence might seem less frightening, more within your power to plan.

▽ Plan for the future. If you have no control whatsoever over your life, or think you don't, then the course of your future must necessarily remain in the dark, too. It's very unsettling not to have any idea what you want to be doing in ten years.

▽ Leave a legacy to your children. If you have the confidence to plan your own life, then you can also plan for your children's future. You may have the self-confidence to concentrate on their moral and ethical training, or you might have the time and energy to try to put something aside to give them a boost financially.

▽ Use your own imagination. The ways in which you change your life are limited only in your mind. You can try one thing—selling your homemade ices to the local gourmet shop—for a while, and test the waters. If it doesn't work out, you can try something else.

▽ Become an expert in something. In addition to experimenting with something new, you can master it—it may be bridge, or growing gourmet vegetables, or woodcarving. It may be a hobby or a new business. It's a wonderful confidence-builder to know that you're the very best in at least one undertaking.

▽ Learn to live in the here and now. Whenever you decide on a new goal, you also have to figure out how to get there. Although it's just great reaching that goal, the getting there—the journey—is the best part of the adventure. It's exciting to be embarked on a new project— learning by doing, succeeding step by step. And, of course, with each successful step, your self-confidence grows and becomes more a part of your basic personality.

▽ Gain real freedom. When you establish goals, and then reach them, your self-esteem soars. With each success, you become more sure of the next success, and you dare to attempt new things.

In managing your life, you can create a masterpiece. You can make it so by shrugging off self-doubt and just getting on with the next interesting project. You cannot help but grow if you continue to take risks and do new things.

Can You Learn Self-Confidence?

Deborah Bright is an author, former diving contestant in the Olympic trials, and president of Bright Enterprises, a company dedicated to helping to enhance the performance of others. Dr. Bright, the author of *Criticism in Your Life. How to Give It, How to Take It, How to Make It Work for You,* knows from her own experience as a competitive diver how easily self-esteem can be shattered and how important confidence is to good performance.

Dr. Bright is another confident woman who believes wholeheartedly in the power of positive thinking. In a sense, if you can think confidently, you will be confident. If you are confident, then you can overcome negative self-absorption and get on with the positive things in your life.

"You can turn your stress into positive energy," says Deborah Bright. "You can actually *learn* to think positively and to direct your energies in productive ways. It's a learned skill. It's not quite like learning to play tennis, but the method of developing good skills and the daily practice are very similar."

When asked how an average woman would develop such skills, Dr. Bright answers: "It's all rooted in an honest evaluation of yourself. You have to work with yourself. And you have to take a hard look at your particular situation and tell yourself the truth.

"Then you should use positive criticism. Rather than beating themselves up emotionally, people who have learned to work with themselves then say, 'Okay, so this is the situation. What am I going to do about it? What can I learn from it?' Then they try to take the problem to the next level, that of solution. And they don't blame themselves for things that they cannot help or control."

We know that willpower is a powerful force and that lack of confidence and shaky self-esteem can be overcome. Every year, when we celebrate with the newly chosen Women of Enterprise, we also recognize someone from our Avon family—someone special who has also overcome great hardship to reach her goals. The winner in 1989 was Aline M. Cadorette, an Avon sales representative from Biddeford, Maine.

In talking about breaking into her sales career, Cadorette remembers: "At first I had no self-confidence and did not feel that I could reach the high goals I saw others achieving. Others encouraged me, and showed me how to set realistic goals. I was determined to be number one, and knew I could do it through hard work and determination."

Aline Cadorette had to overcome more than a lack of self-confidence. In fact, she was painfully shy, and the Quebec-born Canadian spoke almost no English when she first tried to communicate with her new customers in Maine.

Cadorette's early years in this country were hard. She had left a closely knit family in Canada to follow her husband to Maine and help with his trucking business. Her marriage was not a happy one, but the family's Catholicism precluded divorce. Besides, by now she was the mother of two small boys.

To help support the family, Cadorette took a job as a finisher at the local shoe factory. Her home life deteriorated even further as her husband, in 1968, began to suffer from severe headaches, which were accompanied by heavy drinking and increasingly erratic, and dangerous, behavior.

The year 1975 was a watershed year for Aline Cadorette. In July, the shoe factory closed and she no longer had a job. In September, her husband died: his headaches had been caused by the brain tumor that killed him.

With nowhere else to go, Cadorette explored the possibilities of a sales career with Avon. She had tried to sell their products once before, but her very retiring personality and limited English had made it impossible. This attempt, however, was different. She took advantage of the training that Avon offered and learned to set realistic goals for herself.

"In the beginning, I was very scared. My first husband had not been supportive of me and my self-esteem was very poor," says Cadorette. "But when the company's district manager told me she believed in me, I knew there must be something there. I couldn't disappoint her."

Cadorette did very well, establishing a loyal customer base and solid financial independence. She's proud of her new-found self-assurance and credits her Avon experience with helping to develop her potential. And she has a new husband, who enthusiastically supports his wife's thriving business.

As Cadorette succeeded gradually, in small ways, she found that her shyness eased. With each new sale, she gained in self-confidence, and could set more ambitious goals. She recognizes that she has "gained a great deal of self-confidence, learned to take risks, and become very independent."

You, too, can increase your self-esteem, your confidence, in little ways. You will not change overnight, but keep the following list in mind as you try for small successes each day.

1. *Imagine* that you are self-confident. Act out a play in your mind in which you are in command of the situation. If you can imagine forcefully enough, the feeling may very well extend into real life. This is an idea fostered by a lot of people, from Norman Vincent Peale, who calls it "positive imaging," to an English author, Vera Peiffer, who refers to "positive thinking," to a whole group of American thinkers who talk about "visualizations." Perhaps you can think yourself confident.

2. Look at the bright side of things. Be enthusiastic. First, you will cheer yourself up, and, second, you will get a friendlier response from those whom you meet in the course of the day. This is the well-known power of positive thinking. It works. Negative thoughts will just pull you down. To say nothing of depressing everyone around you.

3. Listen, really listen, to those whom you're with. You will learn a lot about how people actually feel, not just how you think they might feel. And you might also learn that your lot is not so awful, after all.

4. If you're not feeling confident about any situa-

tion, try to imagine the worst that can possibly happen. It may not be so awfully bad, and in the meanwhile you haven't wasted a lot of energy worrying.

5. If you're thinking of starting any project, start it today. That diet or painting should not be begun tomorrow, but RIGHT NOW. Because nothing worthwhile ever does get started tomorrow: real projects begin right now.

6. Make lists. You will gain at least the *feeling* of control if you write things down. You could have as many kinds of lists as you feel comfortable with: a list of things to do today, a weekly roundup, and a master list for big projects to complete within the next six months.

7. Start enjoying your life *now*. If you find that your life is a constant round of responsibilities, build in a little time for yourself at once. If you don't often see your spouse, try to make a date with him to go out to dinner; if you need to be alone, plan a movie by yourself. If you can relax, your anxieties will lessen.

8. If you've paid no attention to your physical self in a long time, do so now. Jog. Lose weight. Gain weight if you're too thin. Take tennis lessons. Ask your child to show you how to kick a soccer ball. Borrow her cross-country skis. Just throw a basketball at the hoop in the backyard.

9. Do something—it can be one small thing—that requires a little self-discipline. This can be losing two pounds in a week. It can be repotting all your house plants when you really don't have a green thumb. Just complete any task that you've been promising yourself for months you would get to. You will be amply rewarded with lots of new-minted self-esteem.

10. Make someone else feel good. Take your mother to lunch and the movies. Put in some time at your local hospital. Take the dog for a long walk in the country. Pick up garbage in a park. Baby-sit for some friends and let them take a night off. Selflessness will make you feel better about yourself.

Think about other ways in which you can actively add good things to your life. Your future really is in your own hands. Self-criticism is effective only insofar as it spurs you on to improvement. You've managed to do many wonderful things in your life thus far. You can improve it even more.

4

A WORLD OF POSSIBILITIES

Dreaming about a better future is one of the things that make us human. Wanting more out of life for ourselves and our families is a universal desire. And when we find that we truly want a good life for people whom we don't know—in our community, and country, and around the world—then that raises living on this planet to an art form.

We can help no one until we help ourselves. Until our own lives are in order, we rarely have the interest or the energy to look past our own day-to-day concerns. But when we are contented, and productive, then anything is possible. This is when we are at our best, and somehow find the time to help our families, and friends, and other women, and even people whom we have not yet met.

Possibly by now you have decided that you *do* want to make your life the best it can be—to correct those things that are not working for you and that can be corrected, and to make additions that will add spice—and perhaps cash—to your existence.

In making your life better, it's possible that you may want to make changes in many areas. We are all made up of the physical, the intellectual, and the spiritual—any one of these areas might need work. We find, however, that a real improvement in one of the areas—finding spiritual peace, for example, through a new philosophy, or an interest in serious biking that absolutely transforms you physically—often changes your perspective on life so thoroughly that your relationship to all aspects of your life shifts and adjusts. Such deep-seated change frequently demonstrates that you can do anything you want to do—and your self-esteem soars.

In this chapter, we're going to discuss your intellectual aspect—which is usually demonstrated by the work you do. The physical you will be of concern in chapters 7, 8, and 9, and the spiritual side we will leave to others in your life who specialize in such matters. Getting all three facets of your self together, and moving forward, would be a successful goal for anyone's time on earth.

The Appeal of Adventure

We've talked about control—and the ways in which it might affect your life. The idea of greater control over the day-to-day round is very appealing to many women.

Some of you, though, might be tempted by the song of the open road and the siren call of adventure. If you are within that minority that has no children or other serious encumbrances, like aged parents who need your attention, and your husband, if you have one, is willing to relocate, then you really could seek a new life somewhere else. You could go to another state, like Alaska, or southern California, if you yearn for the warm weather. But it's not always easy to get a job when you don't know the area, and some states are suffering real economic depression. So do your homework first before you hire a van and pack up the furniture and the cat.

You Gotta Know the Territory

Most of you will stay put and deal with the familiar structure of your life. You already know the area in which you live, and to some extent what might be available to you in the economic sector, depending on the direction that you want to take.

What might that direction be?

Corporate America

By "corporate America" we mean those businesses—large or small, publicly owned or family run—that already employ a great many of you. Some of you have worked for such a company for many years, and are happy and feel appreciated; some of you are not so happy, and feel as if you're caught in a rut. Some of you are looking for a job with a local corporation because you want the security of a steady paycheck. And some of you want to work for a company because that's what you did before the kids were born and that's the work world that you know. Now that they're of school age, you feel that you can leave the satisfactions and stresses of child-raising for at least part of the day and return to work.

There are both pluses and minuses about working for one company, in either a full-time or part-time job. Let's review:

THE PLUSES

▽ There *is* that steady paycheck. Whether you get paid weekly, every two weeks, or monthly, you know exactly when it's coming, and for how much. You can plan your budget. This is security, and gives some women a feeling that they have some control over their lives.

▽ You can enjoy the support of others like you on the job. Unless you're stuck alone in a room at a computer terminal all day, or work for a factory whose origins are in the last century along with their employee policies, you probably have the leisure to make friends and enjoy the social give-and-take of the workplace.

▽ Your job may be fun. It may be that you're employed in the design department of a company that manufactures children's clothes. You love to cut out patterns, and work with fabrics. You've been there long enough so that management listens to your opinions, and you have a great deal of job satisfaction.

▽ You have a chance to learn something new, and to make the best use of what you already know. In most corporations, you will advance at least somewhat, even if you're not on the fast track. Hard work and loyalty can be rewarded.

▽ You probably get benefits of various sorts. Some companies are more generous than others when it comes to things like parental leave, vacation policy, and health benefits, but at the very least you should get a basic package of benefits that will cover you and your family. Life insurance, major medical, and hospitalization coverage are absolutely vital.

▽ If you stay with a company long enough, you will often become vested in a pension plan. It's never too early to think about retirement, even if you do not choose to stay with a company forever. But you might as well be smart. If you're vested after five years, for example, it seems foolhardy to leave a job that you might not be wild about after four and a half. Hang in there and get whatever it is that you're entitled to. Then look elsewhere.

THE MINUSES

▽ No job with a corporation is completely guaranteed. Some companies in the United States have come on hard times, and have been facing hostile takeover attempts, and increased competition from Europe and Asia as well as decreased profits. If you *are* employed by a company, it's possible that you may eventually lose your job due to downsizing, or takeover, cost reductions, or reorganization.

▽ When you are a nine-to-fiver, or regular part-timer, your time is *not* your own. You are expected to be on the job according to a prearranged schedule, except for the occasional emergency. That means no sleeping in on a snowy morning because you just feel like it, or working all night because you're feeling creative and energetic, or taking the day off to be a class mother for your child's trip to the zoo.

▽ If your time is not your own, neither, really, is the exact content of your job. You were hired to do certain tasks, which you may or may not have enjoyed, and which may or may not have changed. You must answer to your superiors, and for the most part do the chores assigned to you. Unless you're the boss, you are not autonomous.

▽ The flip side of having satisfying social contact on the job is the possible involvement in office politics, in the strife that sometimes exists in offices or factories or shops. Some work atmospheres are not pleasant—but full of anxiety, self-centered competitiveness, and gossip.

▽ It was popular for a while to think that women were finally coming into their own in the workplace—it seemed that promotions, and wage parity with men, and a wide-open future would be theirs. Although women have certainly made great strides in the workplace, entering middle management in droves in corporations and actually getting hired to do jobs that previously were handed out only to men—construction workers, for example, or firefighters—we do not yet have true equality for women in America's companies and industries. Even today, women are often paid less than men for similar work, are not promoted at the same rate, and are not even considered for some jobs, which are reserved for men.

There Is Another Way

We seem to be experiencing a return to basic values in this country. And some women are rediscovering an earlier pioneer spirit, the idea of doing things for themselves. We have found that we often don't get what we want when we leave our lives in the hands of our parents, our spouses, or the companies that employ us.

As we enter the decade of the nineties, many of us are thinking positively. Sure, there are employment problems in this country. We have all sorts of social and economic difficulties in the United States. Every sector on earth has problems, whether it's the emerging nations of the Third World, or Eastern Europe trying to make its new-found freedoms work, or the industrial countries of the Western World. The modern world has always had troubles of various sorts—war, pestilence, famine, social unrest.

But because times might be hard, that doesn't mean we go to bed and hibernate for our lifetimes. We make the best of opportunities given us. And at this moment in time women in *this* country have all sorts of vistas open to them. There are countless opportunities for employment—in all sorts of traditional and not-so-traditional ways, along avenues other than those laid down by American corporations with their rules and requirements.

With intelligence, and creativity, and a lot of hard work, women can take control of their lives and make them better. None of you should reach the end of your life and think, "Was that it? Why didn't I do more, have more, give more? Was it my fault?" Yes, it can be your fault if you don't jump into your life with both feet and your whole heart and all of your energy.

Are you afraid? Of course you are. Most women contemplating the unknown are. That doesn't mean that they don't take a deep breath and accept the risk.

Others Have Gone Before You

Cynthia DeMonte knows all about the fear of failure. Now president of her own New York City–based marketing and management consulting firm, DeMonte Associates, she became deeply disillusioned with her position in the investment banking division of a major Wall Street brokerage house. Says DeMonte: "Several of the men in my department, all of whom had higher-level jobs, could not express themselves very well. So every time there was a business plan needed, I would redo it, and every time there was a marketing presentation, I would rewrite it. My extra work *was* recognized by the chairman of my department, and he offered me a raise and a promotion. Great news, until I discovered that I would still be making twenty thousand dollars less than any of the men.

"When I questioned him on this, he said, 'As a woman, you should feel lucky that you're given this kind of opportunity on Wall Street. Women on Wall Street are secretaries.' "

That was enough for Cynthia DeMonte, and she decided to try to make it on her own.

"I'll never go to work for another corporation," says DeMonte. "I love the independence and the freedom. You rely only on yourself. You have no one to blame but yourself, and you have no one to reward but yourself. But I *was* desperately afraid when I started out. I was handing out business cards to everyone I knew, my mother was handing them out, and I thought, 'I'm going to get my first client and I'm not going to know what to do. I'm going to fail, and then what am I going to tell people?' But I didn't fail, and the results are worth all that agony."

Among our Women of Enterprise, we have heard hundreds of stories of women who have trusted to the fates and their own abilities. And they have all been afraid to take a chance—they all had a lot to lose. Their courage involved learning to overcome their fear—to control it and make it work for them.

"I wish I could say that I was not afraid, and that I was confident and bold," says Maria Elena Ibañez, founder of a computer business, International Micro Systems, in Miami, Florida, and one of our 1989 Women of Enterprise.

"I have to admit that I was very often afraid," she continues. "But I made it work."

What Maria Elena Ibañez made work is one of the most successful privately held companies in Miami—a company that sells hardware and software for personal computers to her native South America.

Ibañez took many risks to attain her current success. But she had faith in her own ability to succeed and wanted to see how much she could accomplish against great odds.

Born in Colombia, the young Maria Elena Ibañez was exposed to business at a very early age, as she worked summers from the time she was seven at her family's fruit-juice processing plant.

She loved business, and she loved computers. When she was fifteen, the Burroughs Corporation sold ten computers in her home town. Because there was no software available, Burroughs offered a course in computer programming. Ibañez was the only person to complete the course, and she was on her way to learning as much as she could about computers. She recalls with pleasure: "I was the only person in the whole city who knew how to program."

In high school, Ibañez continued with her passion to learn more, and frequently was called upon to develop programs for large corporations. Searching for more sophisticated training, Ibañez transferred to a college in Miami and, after a crash course in English, graduated with honors. She even managed to hold down a job in a campus computer lab.

Ibañez was now ready to take on the computer world. She knew she wanted to start her own business and thought it would be a good commercial idea to develop computer programs in Spanish and market them throughout Central and South America. It was 1979, and she invested $15,000 to start the company she had dreamed of.

Maria Elena Ibañez has always been willing to take a chance on herself, despite fear based on solid knowledge about what *can* happen in the business world. Just five years after her beginnings in 1979, Ibañez managed to transform her fledgling computer business into a $7.5 million enterprise. In 1987, her company was ranked by *Inc.* magazine as one of America's fastest-growing privately held corporations. Today, Ibañez looks confidently to a future managed by her own expertise and positive outlook. "I was determined to be successful," she says. "Nothing stopped me, and I knew that mistakes were only there to help me learn more and more each day. Because of the faith I had in myself, my intuition allowed me to go on, to work hard, to be successful." This is an example of real confidence. There is very little that Ibañez feels she can't handle. Indeed, as a single parent, one of her few real problems is to find enough time to enjoy family life with her two children.

So many of the women whom we meet talk about how they developed increased confidence when they overcame some of life's more tragic events, events that in some cases they never thought they would recover from. The quality of courage that we see when someone bounces back after a disaster, overcomes fear, and goes on to live her life to the fullest inspires all those who hear the story to count their blessings.

Pamela M. Cook, our honorary Women of Enterprise Awards winner for 1987, has that kind of courage. Cook has come a long way in her fifteen years as an Avon sales representative in Charleston, West Virginia.

Cook, a coal miner's daughter, was married to a state trooper in West Virginia when her two-and-a-half-year-old son was diagnosed with leukemia. The boy spent the next six terrible months in a hospital in Cincinnati, with his mother by his side, as doctors tried to save him.

After his death, a grief-stricken Pamela Cook returned to her family in West Virginia and tried to pick up the pieces of her life. She had no college degree, nor any significant work experience. She was afraid that no one would ever hire her, and she wanted badly to supplement her husband's income.

Cook found her answer with Avon. Her sister, an Avon representative in California, suggested that she try selling the products, just to see what the results would be. Cook agreed, but hedged her bets by selling encyclopedias as well. But it was the Avon products that took off—and Cook had found her niche. Not only did she find herself doing very well financially, but she had plenty of time to tend to her family in the way that she wanted.

Pamela Cook is delighted that she had the courage to try something new. The commissions on her six-figure sales have supplemented her husband's income very nicely. Says Cook: "Because of what I earn, my quality of life is so much better. My children have benefited in many ways as a result of the additional income. I have a beautiful home, and my husband is very proud of me."

Money has not been the only benefit enjoyed by Pamela Cook. Over the years, she has developed expert sales skills as well as great poise and an effective professional appearance. Avon suits her way of living, but if she ever cared to change employment, there are many in the Charleston business community who would be enthusiastic about having Pamela Cook join their organization—the offers have been many.

An Abundance of Choices

If you choose to work for a corporation, you no doubt have excellent reasons for doing so. It might be a suitable choice for you now—in time to come you may want to follow a more nontraditional path.

We're seeing the beginning of the age of the entrepreneur, or, to be more accurate, the age of the entrepreneurial woman. According to the United States Small Business Administration, which keeps track of such things, self-employment is expected to rise four times faster among women than among men. They project that the years 1987 to 2000 will see an 83 percent rise in self-employed women, contrasted with an 18 percent rise for the men. In addition, it is projected that by the year 2000 approximately 50 percent of all self-employed entrepreneurs will be women.

Okay, you've thought about it and you're ready to join those millions of self-employed women who are demonstrating how vital they are to the economic well-being of our country, and who are learning to use the resources available to them as they expand.

∇ You want to run your own business.
∇ You want to be answerable only to yourself.
∇ You want to be independent.
∇ You want your time on the job to be flexible, and planned by you.

What do you do now? Where do you look? What fields might be open to you?

Mary Ann Padilla, one of our 1987 Women of Enterprise Awards winners, did what many of you will probably do. She started small, relying on her family for help.

Padilla's family wanted a better life. They migrated from New Mexico to Colorado, hoping for new opportunity. They spoke little English, and were forced to start out as farm laborers. The Padilla children—Mary Ann and her eight brothers and sisters—helped out by topping onions and picking beans. But they stayed in school and got an education.

Mary Ann Padilla managed to complete two years of higher education, at the University of Colorado, and then went to work at a Denver employment agency, where she learned the field. She joined the "character and moral values" of her parents with business knowledge gained on the job and in 1975 opened Sunny Side, Inc., an office personnel service.

Padilla's family helped: she got a loan from a brother, management assistance from a sister, and office decorations and furniture made by her parents.

Her promise is business conducted in a tradition of "quality, reliability, and a sincere sense of service." Today, Mary Ann Padilla employs a staff of six full-time women counselors and maintains a roster of two thousand temporary employees.

Below are some suggestions that can start you thinking about what areas you might pursue. These are just hints to show you the range of possibilities. Your mind and experience are still the best sources of ideas. Only you, for example, are aware that you know how to make absolutely breathtaking silk roses. The next step would be to ask yourself some questions: Do you enjoy making them? Enough to manufacture quite a lot if the orders begin to come in? It's then up to you to scout the sorts of boutiques in your area that might want to sell such items. You would have to do some accounting—and might need some outside advice—to calculate the cost of raw materials, and what you should charge for your time. Do not forget sales tax and overhead. If you still come out ahead, and the project looks promising, then you might be in business and it's time to get expert help.

Your talents, your experience, your knowledge, your interests are the things that come into play in trying to decide a future venture. This is true no matter what your background. American women are as varied as any in the world. Some have been the beneficiaries of advanced education, and a life in which doors have been opened. But sometimes the lives of these women go off course, and they find that they must take care of themselves with very little preparation for the real world. Despite a good education, they may not know how to do anything useful, or practical.

Some women have to get along with very limited formal education. But it's never too late to learn, and there are opportunities that might be yours with just a little training if you fall into that category. For example, perhaps you're very good with your hands and feel comfortable making things. Why not try to find a course in picture framing? Not everyone is capable of cutting glass without also removing a thumb. You might be one of those who could handle it, and it's a craft that pays very well.

Or you might investigate:

Child care. Do you have small children? Would you be willing to introduce other women's children into your home during weekdays? If you love kids, and have the room, you could start your own small day care center. Investigate licensing regulations in your state.

Health care. Once again, you will have to look into the regulations for your state, but it may be that if training is required to be a visiting health care worker, you could get that training. But, in any event, there is always call for workers to come into the homes of the temporarily or chronically ill. If you're not trained in nursing techniques, you could help make the patient comfortable, do the shopping and other chores, prepare meals. With the move to keep patients who don't need constant medical attention at home, not in the hospital, there is usually a need for women who are interested in the helping professions.

Housekeeping and housecleaning. Would you be willing to do for some other family what you've been doing for yours for years? For pay? There are a lot of people out there who are going to offices all day, every day. They frequently need reliable people to come in and perform a variety of tasks: you can often set your own hours as long as the chores are completed. They may range from cleaning, to cooking, to food shopping, to care of a child after school, to picking up items from the cleaners, to waiting for a repairman to arrive—all the things that you're used to doing for yourself and your family.

Yardwork and gardening. Do you know anything about it? If you live in one of our urban areas, you probably don't—but then there would be very little call for such skills. But a lot of women in this country live in suburban areas, or the true country, and may have been born with green thumbs. Work of this sort can range from unskilled labor, which you can do if you're strong and healthy, such as leaf raking and yard cleanup or setting out vegetable beds in the spring. If you're comfortable with plants, there are all sorts of other chores that you can help with that require more training: pruning, dividing plants, planning a flowerbed, choosing and buying seeds and plants, planting trees.

Consulting. This usually builds on work that you've done before, and requires your expert skills. Perhaps you have left a full-time job but want to make use of your contacts, who are potential clients, and keep active part-time while you raise your two-year-old. You think that you will want to return to full-time employment someday and you don't want to get stale. The sort of work that consultants do is as varied as the jobs that are available in corporate America: sales, editorial, public relations, manufacturing, design, accounting, money management, fashion—you name it, and there's a consultant out there who will tell you how to do it better.

Teaching. Do you have a background in teaching? Or would you like to try? "Teaching" can cover anything from part-time substitute in kindergarten (you may have been a full-time teacher at one time) to teacher's aide (for which you need nothing more than a love of children) to college professor in your field of political science to instructor in automotive repair at the local community college adult education center.

You can teach cake decoration at a cooking school or modern dance in your garage or karate or driving or water skiing or sailing or sewing or . . . You fill in the blanks.

Franchising. There are many different kinds of franchises, but in general you pay a large company for the right to use their name. Usually, they will provide training, and materials, and get you started. Franchises might be anything from fast food to a printing company.

Direct sales. This is a great way for women to make some extra money, to get out in the world and meet people, and to develop greater confidence as they learn to run their own small business. A few numbers to spur you on: if you take this route, you'll have lots of company—there are about 4.5 million direct sales representatives in the United States, and 75 percent of *all* U.S. households are contacted by such representatives at one time or another. And of those households, a hefty 50 percent make a purchase. Just make sure the company that you're interested in has a good reputation and you like the product they make.

Sewing and knitting. If you are an expert, then you have something valuable to sell. You can knit sweaters to order, or do alterations, or, if you're really experienced, take orders for upholstery and curtains. How to sell your services? Visit a local knitting shop and see if they need people who can knit to order, or put an ad in your local paper or on a supermarket bulletin board.

Crafts. Do you know how to make charming felt Christmas tree decorations? Or fabric-covered jewelry boxes? Or handmade silk flower arrangements? Do you cover serving trays with shells and then paint them? If your friends love to get your interesting handmade items as gifts, maybe there are potential purchasers out there who would be interested in *buying* them as gifts. Use the same techniques to investigate the market as you would for your knit goods: gift shops, ads in your paper, business cards in local community centers and shopping malls.

Pet care and training. Do you love animals? Do you know a lot about them? There is always a demand for:

∇ Dog walking.
∇ Dog training.
∇ Cat and dog boarding.
∇ Cat and dog care in someone else's home.

A store or restaurant. It is the dream of many an entrepreneur to have a shop or restaurant of her own. The problem with this dream is that, of all our suggestions, this is the one that requires considerable capital. We will discuss the pros and cons of making such an investment in the next chapter, but for now we can say: think about it carefully, make sure you know your business, and then think about it some more. You don't want to lose all your savings in a taco stand that never takes off.

Personal service. The United States is becoming predominantly a service economy. The spectrum of services that is included in this category is so huge that you can surely find a place for yourself in this area if you choose. A service is anything you are able to provide that someone else is unable or unwilling to do for himself or herself—something that person is willing to pay for.

That service might be:

Catering, pet grooming, hairstyling, word processing, driving, videotaping weddings, addressing invitations in your beautiful handwriting, housepainting, floor refinishing, floral arrangements, personal shopping, party planning, and all the thousands of personal tasks that people sometimes have neither the strength, the good health, the time, nor the expertise to do for themselves. There are even services now that will wait in line for you if you're too busy. Need a driver's license? They will go down to the license bureau for you. No time to wait in front of a trendy restaurant that won't take reservations? They will do it.

Look around you. Learn your area. Read your local paper. Talk with shopkeepers. See what's needed, and try to figure out what people are willing to pay for. Dovetail that with what you're willing and able to do, and you're in business. One idea doesn't work? Try another. You are limited only by your energy and imagination.

Try the Experts—Some of Them Are Free

You will have to pay for some of your advice as you learn about entrepreneurism: your accountant, lawyer, possibly an advertising consultant.

But what about the world of information that is there for the taking?

▽ Public libraries. Look in the business section for books about small businesses in general or your idea specifically.

▽ College libraries. Local colleges sometimes allow the public to browse in their libraries. Even if they charge a small fee, it may be worth it to you.

▽ Free lectures or courses sponsored by corporations or business-oriented organizations. If you live in a small town or city, get a schedule of events from your Town Hall or its equivalent. In big cities, companies frequently arrange for lectures on a wide variety of business subjects. Look in the newspaper.

▽ Universities may sponsor lectures that are open to the public. Call the public information office to find out.

You know your own city or town, and you probably know how to find out what's going on. The local newspaper is usually the best source of information, but you could also inquire at your library or chamber of commerce.

Then there is the U.S. Small Business Administration—a government agency supported by your tax dollars and dedicated to serving any small businessperson. Their mandate is to help small businesses become more efficient and profitable.

The Small Business Administration has a broad range of programs and services in more than one hundred locations around the country. Ask about their:

▽ Publications. The SBA has an extensive library of information on most business management topics. The publications usually cost $1.00 or less and are listed in the "Directory of Business Development Publications."

▽ Service Corps of Retired Executives. SCORE is an organization of thirteen thousand volunteers, usually retired businesspeople, who offer management counseling and training.

▽ Small Business Institutes. Under the guidance of a faculty adviser, teams of senior and graduate-level business students will identify management problems, provide long-term, in-depth counseling, and offer specific recommendations to correct problem areas if you've already started a business.

▽ Small Business Development Centers. Services range from prebusiness counseling and training to research and technical advice.

▽ Assistance to women. The SBA has many programs for women entrepreneurs: special outreach for economically disadvantaged women, training in business skills, and counseling programs.

To find out what programs are available in your area, and to get more information about the Small Business Administration, call 1-800-368-5855 or, in Washington, D.C., 653-7561.

The SBA can answer many of your questions before you even start out. Below we'll share some of their recommendations with you.

Questions and Answers About Starting Your Own Business

WHAT IS A BUSINESS PLAN AND WHY DO YOU NEED ONE?

You will probably choose a business that you know something about. A business plan defines your business, identifies your goals, and serves as your company's résumé. It helps you allocate resources properly, handle unforeseen complications, and make the right decisions. Because it provides specific and organized information about your company and how you will repay borrowed money, a good business plan is a crucial part of any loan package.

WHY DO YOU NEED TO DEFINE YOUR BUSINESS IN DETAIL?

Some entrepreneurs have gone broke never answering the question, "What business am I really in?" One watch store owner realized that most of his time was spent repairing watches, not selling them. He finally decided he was in the repair business and discontinued the sales operations. His profits increased dramatically.

WHAT LEGAL ASPECTS DO YOU NEED TO CONSIDER?

Licenses required, zoning laws, and other regulations vary from business to business and from state to state.

93 ❧

Your local SBA office and/or chamber of commerce can give you general information, as can your lawyer. Also ask them which form of organization (sole proprietorship, partnership, or corporation) is for you. Find out about Subchapter S status—it may give you tax benefits.

HOW CAN YOU FIND QUALIFIED EMPLOYEES IF YOU NEED THEM?

Ask friends. Advertise in the newspaper. Put notices up on college bulletin boards if you need part-timers. Some universities have a placement bureau. Try employment agencies as a last resort, as you will have to pay the fee.

Decide beforehand what you want them to do. Be specific. You may need flexible employees who can shift from one task to another. Interview and screen applicants with care.

HOW MUCH SHOULD YOU PAY?

Consult trade associations and your accountant to learn the current practices. Check the newspaper to see what similar jobs are paying in your area. You cannot pay less than the current minimum wage.

IF YOU HAVE EMPLOYEES, WHAT OTHER FINANCIAL RESPONSIBILITIES WILL YOU HAVE?

You must withhold federal and state income taxes, contribute to unemployment and workers' compensation systems, and match Social Security deductions. A good accountant can help you with all of this.

HOW MUCH MONEY DO YOU NEED TO GET STARTED?

It's a good idea to keep your start-up costs as low as possible, which is why many small businesses start at home. If you do rent space, make sure you start with enough capital to cover your building and equipment needs, plus operating expenses for at least a year. These expenses include your salary and money to repay any loans. One of the leading causes of business failure is insufficient start-up capital.

WHAT ARE THE POSSIBILITIES IN FINANCING A BUSINESS?

- ▽ Your own funds.
- ▽ Financial help from spouse or relatives.
- ▽ A partner who will supply some capital.
- ▽ Bank loans.
- ▽ Loans from commercial finance companies, venture capital firms, local development companies, and life insurance companies.

WHAT WILL YOU HAVE TO DO TO GET A LOAN?

You will be asked:

- ▽ How will you use the loan?
- ▽ How much do you need to borrow?
- ▽ How will you repay the loan?

You will have to provide projected financial statements and a cohesive business plan. You will also furnish a description of your experience and management capabilities as well as those of any partners.

WHAT KIND OF PROFITS CAN YOU EXPECT?

It's hard to predict because there are so many variables. But there are standards of comparison called "industry ratios" that can help you estimate your profits. If you're not financially knowledgeable, ask your accountant to look this up for you. These figures are published by several groups and can be found at your library.

WHAT SHOULD YOU KNOW ABOUT
ACCOUNTING AND BOOKKEEPING?

If you don't keep careful records, you won't know how you're doing. At the minimum, it is up to you to substantiate:

- ▽ Your tax returns under federal and state laws, including income tax and Social Security laws.
- ▽ Your request for credit from vendors or a loan from a bank.
- ▽ Your claims about the business, should you wish to sell it.

WHAT FINANCIAL STATEMENTS WILL YOU
NEED?

You should prepare and understand two basic financial statements.

1. The balance sheet, which is a record of assets, liabilities, and capital.

2. The income (profit-and-loss) statement, a summary of your earnings and expenses over a given period of time.

WHAT DOES MARKETING INVOLVE?

Marketing is your most important tool. Think of the four "P's."

1. Product: the item or service you sell.
2. Price: the amount you charge for your service or product.
3. Promote: the ways you inform your market as to who, what, and where you are.
4. Provide: the channels you use to take the product to the customer.

WHAT IS YOUR MARKET POTENTIAL?

The principles of determining market share and market potential are the same for all geographic areas. First determine a customer profile (who) and the geographic size of the market (how many). This is the general market potential. Knowing the number and strength of your competitors (and then estimating the share of business you will take from them) will give you the market potential specific to your enterprise.

HOW DO YOU SET PRICE LEVELS?

The price of a service or item is based on three basic product costs: direct materials, labor, and overhead.

After these costs are determined, a price is then set that will be both profitable and competitive. Pricing can be complicated, so this is an area in which you might consult an expert.

Preparing to Go into Business

The members of the SBA's Service Corps of Retired Executives suggest that their clients complete a check-list at the planning stage. Some of the topics covered are:

IDENTIFYING YOUR REASONS FOR GOING INTO BUSINESS

These include:

- ∇ Freedom from the nine-to-five daily work routine.
- ∇ Being your own boss.
- ∇ Doing what you want when you want.
- ∇ Improving your standard of living.
- ∇ Relief from boredom of present job.
- ∇ You think you have a product or service for which there is a demand.

A SELF-ANALYSIS

Do you have the right personality to become an entrepreneur?

- ∇ Are you a leader?
- ∇ Do you like to make your own decisions?

▽ Do you enjoy competition?

▽ Do you have willpower and self-discipline?

▽ Do you plan ahead?

▽ Do you like people?

▽ Do you get along well with others?

▽ Do you understand that a great deal of hard work will be involved in running your own business?

▽ Do you have the physical stamina to handle the work load?

▽ Do you have the emotional strength to withstand the strain?

▽ Are you prepared, if needed, to temporarily lower your standard of living until your business is firmly established?

▽ Is your family prepared to go along with the strains that they, too, must bear?

▽ Are you prepared to lose your savings?

PERSONAL SKILLS AND EXPERIENCE

▽ Do you know what basic skills you will need in order to have a successful business?

▽ Do you possess those skills?

▽ When hiring personnel, will you be able to determine if the applicants' skills meet the requirements?

▽ Have you ever worked in a managerial or supervisory capacity?

▽ Have you ever worked in a business similar to the one you want to start?

▽ Have you had any business training in school?

▽ If you discover that you don't have the basic

skills needed for your business, will you be willing to delay your plans until you've acquired the necessary skills?

FINDING A NICHE

The most crucial problems you will face in your early planning will be to find your niche and determine the feasibility of your idea. "Getting into the right business at the right time" is very good advice, but following that advice may be difficult. Many entrepreneurs plunge into a business venture so blinded by the dream that they fail to thoroughly evaluate its potential.

IS YOUR IDEA FEASIBLE?

ᐁ Does your product or service satisfy an unfilled need?

ᐁ Will your product or service serve an existing market in which demand exceeds supply?

ᐁ Will your product or service be competitive based on its quality, selection, price, or location?

MARKET ANALYSIS

ᐁ Do you know who your customers will be?

ᐁ Do you understand their needs and desires?

ᐁ Do you know where they live?

ᐁ Will you be offering the kinds of products or services that they will buy?

ᐁ Will your prices be competitive in quality and value?

v Will your promotional program be effective?

v Do you understand how your business compares with your competitors?

v Will your business be conveniently located for the people you plan to serve?

v Will there be adequate parking facilities for the people you plan to serve?

PLANNING YOUR START-UP

v Have you chosen a name?

v Have you chosen to operate as a sole proprietorship, partnership, or corporation? There are legal and tax advantages and disadvantages to each.

v Do you know which licenses and permits you may need to operate your business?

v Do you know the business laws you will have to obey?

v Do you have a lawyer who can advise you and help you with legal papers?

v Are you aware of:

Occupational Safety and Health (OSHA) requirements?

Regulations covering hazardous materials?

Local ordinances covering signs, snow removal, etc.?

Federal Tax Code provisions pertaining to small businesses?

Federal regulations on withholding taxes and Social Security?

State workmen's compensation laws?

SECURITY AND INSURANCE

Have you examined the following categories of risk protection?

▽ Fire
▽ Theft
▽ Robbery
▽ Vandalism
▽ Accident liability

BUSINESS PREMISES AND LOCATION

▽ Have you found a suitable location that is convenient for your customers?
▽ Can the building be modified for your needs at a reasonable cost?
▽ Have you considered renting or leasing with an option to buy?
▽ Will you have a lawyer check the zoning regulations and lease?
▽ If you're going to be working at home, have you investigated tax benefits?

MERCHANDISE

▽ Have you decided what items you will sell or produce, or what services you will provide?
▽ Have you made a merchandise plan based upon estimated sales, to determine the amount of inventory you will need to control purchases?
▽ Have you found reliable suppliers who will assist in the start-up?

▽ Have you compared the prices, quality, and credit terms of suppliers?

BUSINESS RECORDS

▽ Are you prepared to maintain complete records of sales, income and expenses, accounts payable and receivable?
▽ Have you determined how to handle payroll records, tax reports and payments?
▽ Do you know what financial reports should be prepared and how to prepare them?

FINANCES

A large percentage of new businesses fail each year. One of the main reasons is insufficient start-up funds. To avoid this, review your situation by analyzing these three questions.

1. How much money do you have?
2. How much money will you need to start your business?
3. How much money will you need to stay in business?

In calculating number 1, you have to figure out your assets and liabilities.
Assets include:

▽ Cash on hand
▽ Savings accounts
▽ Stock, bonds, securities

▽ Accounts/notes receivable
▽ Real estate
▽ Life insurance (cash value)
▽ Automobile/other vehicle
▽ Other liquid assets

Liabilities include:

▽ Accounts payable
▽ Notes payable
▽ Contracts payable
▽ Taxes
▽ Real estate loans
▽ Other liabilities

Your net worth is your assets minus liabilities.

To estimate the answer to question number 2, How much money will you need to start your business?, think about the following.

Start-up cost estimates include:

▽ Decorating, remodeling
▽ Fixtures, equipment
▽ Installing fixtures, equipment
▽ Service, supplies
▽ Beginning inventory cost
▽ Legal, professional fees
▽ Licenses, permits
▽ Telephone and utility deposits
▽ Insurance
▽ Signs
▽ Advertising for opening
▽ Unanticipated expenses

The third question, How much money will you need to stay in business?, must be divided into two parts: immediate costs and future costs.

Expenses for one month include:

▽ Your living costs
▽ Employee wages
▽ Rent
▽ Advertising
▽ Supplies
▽ Utilities
▽ Insurance
▽ Taxes
▽ Maintenance
▽ Delivery/transportation
▽ Miscellaneous

The total of all these costs will be your operating expenses for one month. Multiply the total by three. That is the amount of cash you will need to cover operating expenses for three months. You ought to have at least this amount in your savings account before opening your business.

To estimate your operating expenses for the first year after start-up, you first have to estimate your sales volume month by month. If you find this sort of projection beyond your current knowledge, consult your accountant, who can probably help—or someone else in the business who wishes you well.

Next, you should determine the cost of goods that will be sold to produce your expected sales (if you're in a service industry, estimate your cost of doing business, including any free-lance help that you might have to hire seasonally).

Your gross is your total net sales minus your costs. Consider also expenses. You have *controllable expenses:*

- ▽ Salaries, wages
- ▽ Payroll taxes
- ▽ Legal/accounting
- ▽ Advertising
- ▽ Automobile
- ▽ Office supplies
- ▽ Dues/subscriptions
- ▽ Telephone
- ▽ Utilities
- ▽ Miscellaneous

and *fixed expenses:*

- ▽ Rent
- ▽ Depreciation
- ▽ Insurance
- ▽ Licenses/permits
- ▽ Taxes
- ▽ Loan payments

All expenses added together and subtracted from total income equal your before-tax profit or loss.

WHAT IF YOU WANT TO BORROW MONEY?

You may have already discovered that it's difficult for women to borrow money, even if they enjoy excellent credit-worthiness. Make sure that if you approach a bank or other lending institution, your information is complete and correct. The banker will want to know . . .

▽ What sort of person you are. Have you managed a business before? What is your credit history?
▽ When and how you plan to pay back the loan.
▽ If you've asked for enough money to make allowance for unexpected developments.
▽ What the outlook is for your type of business or industry in general.
▽ If your financial statement is adequate to give him or her a complete picture.
▽ If you understand the different types of loans available: short term, term money, and equity capital. These are funds to be used for different purposes and paid back from different sources. Consult your accountant if you are not familiar with these terms.
▽ What collateral you can offer. Sometimes you can get a friend, relative, or business partner to sign a note. Or you can pledge your stock of goods if you're in manufacturing, or delivery trucks, or equipment. Real estate might also be acceptable, stocks and bonds, or life insurance. Be sure that you can afford to lose whatever it is that you're offering. And be sure you understand the terms of the loan. It's a good idea to have your lawyer or accountant visit the lending officer with you. You must be absolutely clear about the repayment terms.

There are a lot of terms and concepts in the above lists. You don't have to understand them all at the very beginning of your venture. That's why you will have an accountant and lawyer to help you. But you do have to understand the product or service that you're offering. The creative part is up to you or your partner. You are the ones who will furnish the idea, the enthusiasm, and the certainty that there is a waiting market. The vision must be yours, as well as the belief that you will succeed.

5

THE REALITY FACTOR

"**I**f you think you can do it, you can!" says Terry Engebretson, an Avon sales representative from Redwood City, California, and a 1988 Women of Enterprise honorary award winner. By "it," Engebretson means trying for a good life and succeeding. "It has been my dream to be successful and happy, and I believe I have accomplished both," she says today.

And, yet, seventeen years ago Terry Engebretson was not feeling so positive. She had been abandoned by her husband, who gave her minimal child support for the two children and no alimony. Engebretson had few marketable career skills. While supporting herself and her children by clerking at a law firm, she started selling Avon products part-time to help pay her bills. Although during her lunch hours she rang doorbells in the traditional way, Engebretson was quick to realize that a lot of women who used to be home to answer those doors were now in the workplace. She asked customers who worked in offices and factories to distribute Avon catalogues at their jobs. The system was efficient, and sales at the workplace soon accounted for 50 percent of her income. "Business is where the real money is," she notes.

Terry Engebretson became a full-time sales representative in 1983 and hasn't looked back since. She has the right kind of personality for sales, with plenty of self-confidence. She's well organized and an enthusiastic self-starter and enjoys competing with herself by "setting my own goals and achieving them! . . . Avon has changed my life. I've had an opportunity to meet wonderful people, and to earn more money than I ever dreamed possible. I finally feel like I am somebody."

Terry Engebretson has found her niche. She's gotten her life in order and she's found a way of making a living that suits her. She's her own boss. A lot of women agree with Terry Engebretson as they search for independence and control. A report in a *Wall Street Journal* of a few years ago summarized a survey in which women were asked to name their dream job—what they would do if they had a choice: "The response? Overwhelmingly, women said they'd like to run their own business."

That answer would still be true today, as we enter into the 1990s. Being your own boss, directing your own destiny, controlling your own time on the job, are all very attractive concepts. But is the life of an entrepreneur right for you? We think it's a good choice for a great many women—but it's not for everyone. Or it may not be for some people right *now*. People change, and they grow, as they meet new experiences. Sometimes one has to develop the ability to take risks.

We'd like to ask some questions in this chapter. You'd probably like to know (1) *who* is the right sort of person to take a chance on her own creativity and energy, and (2) *why* people are willing to put up with the financial uncertainty of entrepreneurship, and (3) *how,* if you're willing to take the plunge, you go about it.

Who Are the Risk Takers?

We'd like you to ask yourself some questions, too. You'd probably enjoy having greater control over your existence. Most people do. Trying to establish an economic life you can manage yourself is one way to get that control. But it may be that you're not sure. You have to think about what *you* are like, what you want— not your mother, or your sister, or your best friend. You might be more comfortable within the structure of a nine-to-five job, or not working at all, if you don't have to. But maybe you just need to stop agonizing about whether to make a change or not, and just do it. Let's see if you're ready.

The quiz below has no right or wrong answers. Your score will simply indicate whether you're in the right frame of mind to sail out on your own into uncharted waters, or whether you still should remain in the more predictable harbor of full-time employment with a boss other than yourself.

Am I Ready to Be My Own Boss?

Please circle the answer that most nearly fits the way you feel today. See the end of the quiz for your score.

1. I have a reasonable amount of confidence when:
    a. I'm in a familiar situation, and doing tasks that I've done before.
    b. I'm in a completely new situation. In fact, I see it as a challenge and enjoy the excitement.
    c. Never. I can't seem to get my act together and usually approach any situation with anxiety.
2. I'm in a competitive situation. I:
    a. Think only of winning. I will do anything within reason and my code of ethics to come out on top.
    b. Would like to win, but I'm much more interested in the competition as a learning experience.
    c. Don't mind winning, but sometimes I care more about other things.
3. When I start a project, even if it's just filing all the recipes I've cut out of magazines over the years:
    a. I figure I'll finish it someday.
    b. I'll complete it by next Christmas, when we have lots of company and I'll need the bed that they're piled on.
    c. I make a schedule and stick to it. Nothing ever takes more than a few weeks.

4. I'm faced with a suggestion that carries some risk (my brother-in-law wants to be partners in a land speculation deal):

    a. I tell my brother-in-law that my husband and I will discuss it and let him know in a week or so.

    b. Yes, yes, yes! The only way to make money is to spend it.

    c. No, no, no! A fool and her money are soon parted.

5. When I have to come up with an original idea, whether it's a theme for a shop window or a costume for my six-year-old:

    a. My costume is up to Broadway show standards.

    b. My costume is okay, except that another child also came as Frosty the Snowman.

    c. I buy a costume at the five-and-ten. You can't have too many Batmen.

6. I decide that I really need to lose five pounds:

    a. I gain at least three, because I'm thinking of food all the time.

    b. I lose six, just to be sure.

    c. Nothing happens, and then I lose interest.

7. When it comes to being a self-starter:

    a. There is no job that I can't plan by myself, and see it through as well.

    b. I really am uncomfortable unless I have someone to give me a clear idea of the task before I begin.

    c. I can get started okay, but then I like to have someone fill in the bits and pieces that I've forgotten.

8. If there's a crisis at work or at home, and I have to put in long, stressful hours, I find that:
    a. I have plenty of energy, and always get through in good shape.
    b. I manage to stay on my feet, but just barely.
    c. I usually have to turn to a colleague or relative to help out.

9. When it comes to meeting and greeting, I am:
    a. Shy enough to try to get someone else to handle the social/business chores.
    b. Reasonably capable. I get knots in my stomach when, for example, I have to give a presentation at work, but I manage.
    c. Definitely a people person. I love to meet and greet.

10. My word is:
    a. My bond. I consider a handshake as binding as a written contract.
    b. Variable. I try to stay on the straight and narrow, but sometimes you have to cut corners to make a profit.
    c. Not very good, but in business you have to look out for yourself.

11. Someone has to take charge of a project at work. Whoever gets the nod will be in charge of a team of ten. I:
    a. Hope that it will be my closest friend at the office because she'll give me an interesting assignment.
    b. Desperately want the job myself. I know just how I'll manage it. I put in a bid with my supervisor.

    c. Would like to be in charge, but don't know how to speak up.

12. When things don't go my way:

    a. I write it off to experience and learn from the failure. Next time I'm confident that I'll do better.

    b. I become wildly discouraged and sulk for days.

    c. I'm quite disappointed and try to explain it away. I might blame someone else.

13. When I'm presented with the opportunity to learn something new—a course in a new technology, for example—I:

    a. Snap it up no matter what adjustments I have to make to my schedule. You never know when a new skill will come in handy.

    b. Try to join in if it's convenient. It frequently is not convenient as I'm very, very busy.

    c. Hardly ever have time unless my boss clearly is very anxious to have me do it.

14. Ever since I was a little girl, people have told me that I'm very:

    a. Flexible, perhaps even wishy-washy.

    b. Rigid and unbending.

    c. Sure of myself, although always willing to listen to an expert opinion.

15. I have an idea for a small business—a gardening center in the suburban community in which I live. I love flowers and plants and:

    a. I know all about them.

    b. I can barely tell a rose from a daffodil, especially if they're both yellow.

c. I know only a little, but I'm willing to learn by apprenticing myself to an expert.

Scoring: Find the point value for each answer. Then add up your points.

1. a = 2, b = 3, c = 1
2. a = 3, b = 2, c = 1
3. a = 1, b = 2, c = 3
4. a = 2, b = 3, c = 1
5. a = 3, b = 2, c = 1
6. a = 1, b = 3, c = 2
7. a = 3, b = 1, c = 2
8. a = 3, b = 2, c = 1
9. a = 1, b = 2, c = 3
10. a = 3, b = 2, c = 1
11. a = 1, b = 3, c = 2
12. a = 3, b = 1, c = 2
13. a = 3, b = 2, c = 1
14. a = 2, b = 1, c = 3
15. a = 3, b = 1, c = 2

How You Rate: Are You Ready to Be Your Own Boss?

A Captain of Industry (45–38 points): You are surely ready. You have confidence, and enthusiasm, and creativity. You seem to be absolutely ready to control your own life, and to shape it in any way that you want. Go for it!

On the Brink (37–26 points): The desire for an entrepreneurial lifestyle, and control over that lifestyle, is there, but you need to work on your self-esteem.

Perhaps you could start gradually. Get a part-time job in a field that interests you and see where that takes you by this time next year.

Needs Work (25–15 points): You may want to try to go out on your own, but it's dangerous for you to try your wings just now. Analyze in what areas you are most insecure and then work on them. For instance, there are many techniques that you could try. Setting small goals and rewarding yourself for modest successes are frequently confidence builders.

You might try a helpful course or two. Some quite shy people, for example, profit enormously from public speaking instruction. It may seem terrifying at first, but remember that everyone else in the course is just as scared as you are. And the benefits can be immeasurable. Women tell us that once they learn to feel comfortable in front of a group, then nothing else that comes up in business seems hard to handle.

Why Do You Want to Be an Entrepreneur?

We hope that if you really want to try some sort of business of your own, that your scores show you to be the possessor of solid self-esteem, a risk-taker, someone who has faith in her own abilities. You can learn to recognize obstacles and overcome them. No new venture will be trouble-free. Prepare yourself for difficulty ahead of time. If trouble comes, do not panic. Consult with your spouse, your partners or other advisers, and exercise damage control. There will be a solution to most of the problems that you might face.

Madeleine Swain, co-chair and president of Swain & Swain, a corporate outplacement and management consulting firm, often helps clients who have left corporations start their own businesses. In a speech at a conference sponsored by the Entrepreneurial Women's Network, Swain said, "In my experience, and through the experience of women I have counseled over the years, I've found adversity often has played a role in the initial decision and ultimate success of one's venture. Women have often embarked upon the decision of self-employment through some rather inauspicious beginnings—being fired from a corporate job not being an uncommon one at all.

"If we agree that the entrepreneurial spirit is captured by an opportunistic sense—seizing the moment—what really matters is what we do with the challenges that face us: a lost job, the frustration of an unfulfilling career, the desire for more control over one's own destiny. . . . Research has shown that women are more likely to move in new and original directions than men . . . and are being forced to approach situations from a new and different perspective."

Women sometimes do feel left out of the man's world that they often encounter in the workplace. And if they recognize their own abilities, they want the same unlimited opportunities that their male counterparts enjoy. It seems, though, that although women become entrepreneurs certainly for a chance at greater financial gain, equally important is the increased control over their personal and work lives.

We have seen that among the reasons for women seeking some sort of nontraditional employment are:

∇ The chance of making more money. When you're in business for yourself, your only limitation is your ability to intelligently market whatever goods or services you're selling.

∇ Necessity. Some women are fired. Some women lose spouses. Some families suffer financial reversals. Women in these situations try to make as much money as possible doing what they know how to do.

∇ No marketable skills. Corporations can be quite rigid in their requirements. Willingness to work hard and the knowledge that one has enough intelligence to be trained are often not enough for a woman to find a job. And, yet, if a woman has confidence in her abilities and *knows* that she can figure out the hard stuff, and do a good day's work, sometimes the only outlet for these abilities is for a woman to become her own employer.

∇ The desire for more control over what you do, how you do it, and when you do it. The woman entrepreneur, especially if she works at home, can establish a flexible schedule to include household duties as well as her new business.

∇ Excitement. Some women are just thrilled by a challenge. The idea of creating a concept, bringing it to life, and making sure that it's successful can make some women very happy, and it's often true that their enthusiasm and attention to detail all add up to a successful business.

∇ Problems with just being a woman. Some fields are still male-dominated, and women don't see why. They want a piece of the pie, too, and are willing to put themselves in business to try and compete.

The above are not the only reasons that women go into business for themselves, whether the business is a shop, or direct selling, or consulting, or running a dinner theater in an old barn. There are as many reasons as there are women who have a dream. They all want to be their own boss. They all want independence, to be creative, to plan their own time and make their own work decisions without having to answer to superiors. They all want the freedom to fly as high as their abilities will carry them.

How Do You Learn the Ropes?

An enormous percentage of new entrepreneurs fail the first time out (as many as four out of five within the first five years)—we don't want you to be included in that statistic. We think that with determination, hard work, a little luck, and a realistic assessment of the marketplace you can number among the many success stories.

YuVonne Hoovestal, president of Greenway Enterprises, a construction company in Helena, Montana, and a 1989 Women of Enterprise, did not fail.

Hoovestal was born on an Indian reservation, a member of the Gros Ventre tribe. Her father was the Indian chief of police, and her mother was a dietitian. Early on, they stressed the value of hard work. By the eighth grade, Hoovestal was attending public high school. and having to make her way among the local white children. It was her first experience with prejudice. And it was the beginning of her determination to overcome all odds to help make a better life for herself.

By the time she was in her twenties, that goal had begun to become reality. At nineteen, Hoovestal had married a white man and had helped put him through college. In 1978, ever on the lookout for an economic challenge, Hooevestal, while working as an office manager for a dental surgeon, focused on the concept of "hydroseeding," a little-known but effective method of lawn cultivation. The fledgling business came to life at the kitchen table in the evenings.

YuVonne Hoovestal had a gift for marketing her product: "I'd identify the best property in a neighborhood and persuade the owners to let us put in a free lawn," she recalls. "Pretty soon, everyone else wanted one, too."

The business gradually evolved to include construction jobs, which soon became the main focus for Hoovestal and her husband, who in 1985 left teaching to join his wife. Today, Greenway Enterprises is a successful construction company that has built all sorts of projects—highways, bridges, water and sewer lines, industrial and commercial buildings—throughout a five-state region.

It hasn't been easy: Hooevestal, who is forty-eight, has had the double-barreled problem of being a Native American in Montana, and a woman in the male-dominated field of heavy construction. "Indians are not well accepted in the Montana business community," she says. "Overcoming this stigma with bankers has been difficult. I have to prove myself in each new business situation. . . . But for an Indian girl to have reached this level of business success is beyond my wildest expectations."

YuVonne Hoovestal gives us some insight into her ability to focus on a goal and gain that goal when she says, "I often thought about the glory that used to be part of the American Indian culture. As a descendant of those who lived that glorious past, I always thought I was destined to choose many things and to be successful. I always knew I had potential for success if I didn't give up. . . . I have learned to do battle in the white society. I strive to serve as an example of our potential for victory. . . . My message is, if I can do it, anyone can. If you just decide that *you* will never give up. To paraphrase Chief Joseph of the Nez Percé tribe, I say, I will fight for evermore and win."

How Will Your Business Grow?

The fact alone of going into business for yourself proves that you are willing to take risks. For your business to grow and prosper, you must be prepared to encounter difficulties.

If you learn to overcome them, and persevere, you will succeed. If you take a risk, and fall on your face, you won't fall apart. Men have taken risks in their careers for generations, and we must learn to take them, too.

First, don't be afraid of calculated risks. Calculated means carefully considered. If you're trying to make a decision about an important but risky step, ask yourself first, "What is the *worst* thing that can happen?" If you're not willing to live with whatever your answer is, don't take the chance. Then ask, "How much of a risk can I afford to take at this time in my life?" If you can't afford to lose anything, stop right there.

Try putting the pros and cons down on paper in two separate columns. What do you have to lose, and what do you have to gain? What are the odds on each side? What strengths and experience do you bring to this venture? What weaknesses? What unexpected factors beyond your control could change the outcome?

Weigh risk versus reward. You don't have to do this scientifically. The main value of the exercise is to crystallize the issues in your mind. Sometimes the very act of writing down an unpleasant possibility—or a pleasant one—helps you make the final decision with your nerve as well as your brain. When you take a risk, don't be terrified of losing. In any game where there are winners, there will be losers. It's not a disgrace. Learn from the experience. You will win next time.

Women who consider entrepreneurship should think long-term, because most successful companies do not even begin to grow until after their first four years. It's easy to become discouraged when you're working an eighteen-hour day and see no real progress. You're not trying a get-rich-quick scheme, but should be prepared for a slow, steady climb. If you're prepared for an uphill struggle, the odds are in favor of your getting where you want to go.

How big do you want to be? Not every business has to grow to mammoth proportions. For some, success means a small but mature company, operating with limited staff, minimum overhead, and maximum profits. For others, the dream is a full-scale operation. But with growth come more expenses and greater risk. How much are you willing to risk? Are the rewards worth it?

As your fledgling business sprouts wings and begins to fly, it will cross a faint but unmistakable line between start-up and revved up. This has begun to happen to many of the companies that started within the last ten years, during our national entrepreneurship boom. Companies in general are becoming smaller and less hierarchal, more entrepreneurial in spirit. Many more companies are giving their employees a percentage of the profits. And companies must be willing to work cooperatively within a network of other companies—venture partners, suppliers, customers. They are becoming concerned with more than the bottom line—with quality and service.

Twenty-five Tried and True Tips—A Review

Although every woman's experience, background, needs, ambitions for economic self-determination differ, there are some ideas that we'd like to share with you if you're thinking about entrepreneurship. We've discussed some of these earlier—use these tips as a checklist before making any final decisions.

1. *Do what you know how to do*. This may be knowledge gained from an office job—consulting, word processing. It may be a hobby—old car restoration. It may be an extension of your household skills—

you bake the best strawberry pie in the world. But you're going to be busy learning how to run a business, so it's not a good idea to have to learn about what you're doing as well.

2. *Define your business idea.* Before you invest time and money, be sure you have a firm grip on your idea. It's not enough to say, "I'm going to be a caterer." What is your market? Business groups? Can you feed forty, or is eight your limit? Do you have someone to help you? Does your community have a lot of elderly couples who might be grateful for someone to come in and cook a meal a few times a week? Do your research before you even dream of disarranging your family's schedule.

3. *Be prepared to work hard.* Going into business for yourself? Prepare to work as hard as you've ever worked in your life. If a problem arises, you have to stay up until you've figured out a solution. This is a time to take good care of yourself. Be sure you eat, try to find time to exercise, and take care of yourself physically.

4. *Learn to take final responsibility.* The buck definitely stops with you. If you have never been able to make decisions, you are not the right sort of personality to run a business. You must make them, and you must make them quickly. And if things don't work out, you take the heat.

5. *You need a real business plan.* If you don't know how to go about it, you might need professional help. There are books on the market that will help. You should estimate how much business you think you can attract, what you can charge, what your start-up

costs might be, how much you will pay your consulting experts and any employees, overhead costs, taxes—and any expected profit.

6. *Hire experts.* Unless *you* are an expert in either legal or money matters, you ought to have a lawyer and an accountant before you even get started. Try to stay away from friends and family, unless your son is just out of law school and you have absolutely no money to hire a stranger. When you mix your business and personal life, it often ends badly.

You need to talk to a lawyer to decide which of the three kinds of business structure you think would be best for you: if you're alone, a sole proprietorship would be suitable; if you have partners, and are contemplating the kind of business in which lawsuits would be unlikely to occur, then a partnership might be the answer; but if you will be working with others, and any of you has considerable personal property, like a house, it might be wise to spend the extra money to incorporate—in that case, your personal property cannot be touched in case of legal unpleasantness.

And unless you are fiscally knowledgeable, it is good business to talk to an accountant before you spend your first dollar. Go over your business plan with this person, and have him or her help you set up an efficient way to keep your books, as well as estimate for you what your first-year expenses, including taxes, are likely to be.

Try to choose a lawyer and an accountant who are helpful and whom you like. You need to learn a great deal from these people at the beginning. It would be ideal to find intelligent, conscientious young people who are just starting out and who are willing to grow along with your business. You don't want to find yourself trying desperately to get an answer from an accountant who is much too busy to return your calls.

In time, there are other experts whom you might need to consult: a banker, for example, if the time comes for some financing, or a publicist or public relations person, if you need advice about possible advertising. It's early days yet, but keep in mind that these services exist to help you expand.

7. *Start small*. For a start-up business, unless your clientele is going to be very fancy indeed (which *might* be true if you're going to try your hand at catering), you don't need engraved business cards, or two-color letterhead. And don't buy a copier or fax machine until you see that you really can't get along without it. Start small, buy only those supplies that you need right away, keep your overhead low.

8. *Keep regular business hours if you work at home*. Clients should know that they can get you during the workday—if you must go out for an appointment, whether business or personal, you will, of course, have an answering machine to field calls, with a very businesslike message on it. *You* record the message—it is not amusing to let the children do it.

9. *Dress in an appropriate way, even if you're working in the laundry room*. A workday is a workday. You should be dressed in business clothes—you never know when a client will drop by or you will have to dash to an unexpected meeting. This doesn't necessarily mean high heels, full makeup, and earrings—but you don't want to be caught in your pajamas at eleven o'clock in the morning.

Also, your frame of mind will be more work-oriented if you're not making business calls in jeans and sneakers.

10. *If you have small children, arrange for appropriate child care.* Yes, you can pick your kids up at school—after all, being with them and caring for them is one of the reasons for being in business for yourself. But you cannot really be both an effective full-time mom and a full-time, or even part-time, businessperson. You must have some hours for yourself—to call clients, to get your books in order, just to think. You can't do that if you have a two-year-old and a four-year-old tugging at your hem. Try to get someone to help you for at least a few hours a day.

11. *Organize your time.* Before you jump into a new enterprise full-time, review your responsibilities. Do you have a family? Elderly parents? Some realignment of tasks might be necessary. Clearly, you can't abruptly leave those who rely on you to fend for themselves. You may need to make schedules of who does what, when.

12. *If you have a family, learn how to focus on their needs and fulfill your responsibilities.* If you have a spouse and children, and you work as a nine-to-fiver, you have to take careful control of your life.

Make lists. You must learn to focus on what's necessary, and not deplete your store of energy pointlessly. You can use downtime at the office to think about family matters: plan your daughter's birthday party, for example.

Make use of your lunch break. This may be the only time to buy sneakers for your twelve-year-old.

If you find that holding a full-time job and giving your family the attention they need is too much at this point in your life—your children might be quite young, for example—then consider your alternatives:

Part-time work.

Employment with a company that offers flextime. Perhaps you could work from seven to three, and be home when your children arrive from school. This might work well if your husband could see that the kids get off to school in good shape.

Work at home. With the spread of computers, there are new opportunities for those who are computer-literate or willing to learn. Or you could try some of the entrepreneurial ideas that we have suggested earlier.

Whatever you decide, your goal should be a well-balanced life. You need a satisfying occupation, and time to care for and enjoy your family. Don't forget you: you deserve care also. You need time to yourself, to exercise, read, think, keep your wardrobe in order—all those details that go into your looking good and feeling great.

13. *Organize your space and your equipment.* You need a place to work that is yours alone. This can be a desk in a corner of the kitchen, but you should have easy access to a telephone and any other equipment that you will need. You want to avoid at all costs having to gather up every scrap of work-related material at the end of the workday.

Don't invest in too much equipment—you can't be sure at the beginning what you will need—but there are necessary basics: ledgers, notebooks, file folders, file cabinets, office sundries like paper clips, rubberbands, pencils, typewriter or computer. You need enough to keep your projects easily organized.

14. *Include family and friends in your planning.* Any entrepreneurial venture is bound to cause upheaval in your life, and your family's. You want to make sure that those near and dear to you are included for two very important reasons.

First, and most important, you're going to be undergoing some stress as you try something new, and their love and support are going to be vital to your well-being. It's always more comforting to be able to think that "We're all in this together." If you share your dreams, your fears, as well as day-to-day problems, you will not feel alone. And how might those closest to you feel about a new venture? They would probably choose to share your ups and downs—after all, they're part of your life.

Second, friends and family are often a source of practical, as well as emotional, support. Does your mother have a lot of free time? Perhaps she'd be willing to watch the kids a few afternoons a week, or make some follow-up phone calls, or address envelopes. Your best friend? Maybe she wouldn't mind calling her cousin the paper merchant to see if you can get a good price on business stationery. Your husband? If you're successful enough, perhaps you could work together and really get the business off the ground.

15. *Keep learning.* No matter what your field, get as much information as you can from whatever sources are available. These might be business-sponsored seminars, or new books in your field, or courses taught by experts at a high school or community college. Ap-

prenticeships are still possible. If your dream is to run an antiques shop, then work in one for six months. Learn by doing.

16. *Learn about the territory and your potential market.* Are you opening a shop? Spend hours at the potential location, just hanging out on the street corner. Observe traffic patterns. What shop windows do the passersby look into? Are there *a lot* of passersby? If not, go elsewhere. And talk to other shopkeepers. There are some locations in otherwise busy areas that are just death. No one knows why, but you don't want to be stuck with them. You can learn which these are by asking about the store turnover during the past few years.

Do you want to sell your custom-made sweaters? Go into a boutique and see what people in your area are really buying. And how much they're willing to spend. Obviously, if you live in a depressed mining area in Pennsylvania, it is not a good idea to specialize in cashmere pullovers—simple, serviceable, warm wool sweaters might be the ticket.

17. *Do you face any real competition?* Are there local businesses or services that are similar to yours? If so, are they successful? Can the market support another one? And what can you offer that your competition cannot?

18. *Watch for clever ways to advertise your product or service.* Even at the beginning, you will probably advertise at least a little. You have to tell people that you are selling something worth buying. As time goes on, you may have more money to spend on advertising and perhaps even public relations, which tries to put your name forward in ways that are not out-and-out

advertising, a news piece in the local paper, for example.

19. *Learn to share the risks.* Get help. Earlier, we discussed the popularity of the Horatio Alger concept in this country. All of this best-selling author's heroes had the help of a rich and powerful mentor, someone who recognized the hero's good qualities and helped him in a selfless way. It sometimes helps to find that sort of mentor, someone to share the risks, or someone who can be a sounding board, and who can give you reliable advice.

There are many organizations that supply sales training. These are usually large corporations that not only furnish training, but also materials and enough basic information so that anyone with drive and ambition can get started in sales. Just make sure that the company you choose has a good track record—talk with people who have worked for them—and that you like the product that you will be selling.

And there are other ways to share the risks. Madeleine Swain, president of the management consulting firm of Swain & Swain, is the co-author with Robert Swain of *Out the Organization: How Fast Could You Find a New Job?* The Swains coin the word "midpreneur" in this book, meaning a "risk taker, but somewhat more cautious. The midpreneur . . . will perhaps adapt an existing idea, or continue to expand a business found to be successful.

"Key to a midpreneur's operation is sharing the risk. This is a reactive individual, who looks about in the surrounding commercial milieu and sees an idea that can be modified, expanded, transformed in some way to their benefit."

Ways of sharing the risk include having partners, making sure that no matter what the endeavour your monetary investment is very small—"sweat equity" is the term used when your greatest investment is hard work.

Whether you're doing business with a client or a supplier, or working with a partner or employee, it's much more gratifying to share the experience with someone whom you like and trust. The establishing of loyal friendships is one of the benefits of the work world. You meet lots of people, and some of them will become companions for life.

20. *Learn about money.* Nobody expects you to know all about finance when you're just starting out. But this is one area in which you should become knowledgeable. First, you want to be able to understand what your accountant is telling you. Second, you will never be able to expand if you don't know how to deal with banks and other lending institutions. You have to figure out if you are credit-worthy, and how to convince banks that you are a good risk.

How do you do this?

You talk to people: your accountant, for example. We mentioned earlier that your accountant should not be so grand that he or she cannot return your calls for three days. You need to pick this person's brains at the beginning, and he or she should be anxious to grow along with you. You can talk to banks. They have information officers who specialize in small businesses. Ask questions.

Many cities have service organizations staffed by retired businesspeople. The U.S. Small Business Administration, for example, supplies this sort of aid.

There is usually no charge for a consultation, or it is minimal. These people are worth their weight in gold—find out if your town or city has such a service.

You take courses. Yes, just like going back to school. Except that this information has to do with real life. And the rules that you learn can be applied to making your livelihood better.

You read books. There are thousands of books offering advice to entrepreneurs in every conceivable kind of business. You don't even have to buy them. Go to your public library or ask to use the business section of your local college if there is one.

21. *Consider buying an established business.* This will save you the time and expense of starting from scratch. But:

Be sure you know something about it. It would be useful if the previous owner would stay around for a while to train you.

Find out as much about the business and the previous owner as you can. Does he or she have a good reputation? If it's a shop, is it in a busy location? Have there been any changes that might cause the previous owner to want to sell? Be very careful, and make sure your accountant does a careful audit. You don't want to buy a small gourmet food shop only to discover that the supermarket a block away is putting in a new line of fancy foods.

If it's a store, find out about the lease. Has the owner of the building been tripling the rent when other leases come up for renewal? Has the composition of the neighborhood changed so much that your usual clientele has all moved away?

22. *Invest in a franchise.* These are usually individually owned businesses that are operated as if they were part of a large chain. You use the franchise owner's name, reputation, and often product.

Advantages:

You will get training from people who have had a lot of experience.

You will have lower start-up costs than if you did it yourself.

You will inherit an established image.

You will probably enjoy the savings that come with chain purchasing power.

Disadvantages:

You will probably have to do it their way.

You will have to share the profits.

You may inherit problems peculiar to the franchise owner.

You will have to produce time-consuming reports.

If your franchiser fails, so will you.

23. *If you have employees, you have added responsibilities.* If you have to hire people, you become a boss. You will have to think about job descriptions, and promotions, and raises, and firings. Also, you have to consider their welfare. If they give you their loyalty, they will expect it in return. That means you cannot decide to close down for three months because you have an opportunity to accompany your husband to Paris.

24. *If you are a member of a minority, check to see if there are any special assistance programs that might help you.* You might be the member of a racial or ethnic minority, or have a physical handicap, or

perhaps can qualify just because you're a woman. Check with your local chamber of commerce—every area in the country has different opportunities.

25. *Learn how to deal with stress.* Anyone starting a new venture suffers from stress—from anxiety, exhaustion, uncertainty. You want this to be an exciting time for you and your family. You certainly don't want to make your life *worse.*

Try to put aside special time for your spouse and children. Although this may never have come up before, you may actually have to plan ahead for time together.

Take care of yourself and make time for yourself. Sleep, exercise, eat properly. This is one time when you might consider joining a dance group or exercise class away from home. You might find that you need some structure not imposed by yourself, and getting out of the house could be an added bonus if you're running a business from your kitchen table.

If things get to be too much for you, don't keep it to yourself. Talk to your business partner if you have one, or your spouse, or your mother or best friend. Vent. Talk it out. You no longer have that built-in support group that you had in your last office job. You have to make your own.

Whatever path you choose, don't be discouraged if things are a little rocky at first. So many of our Women of Enterprise mention perseverance, and belief in their own abilities, as bedrock to success. And as YuVonne Hoovestal says, "If I can do it, anyone can. If you just decide that you will never give up."

6

ARE YOU READY FOR
THE FUTURE?

There are some rules of human conduct that have come down through the centuries that are often referred to as "truths." In fact, they *are* true. One is the golden mean, which suggests that we be moderate in all things. The other is the golden rule: "Do unto others as you would have others do unto you."

As you decide what direction you would like your life to take from now on—what changes are important for you to make so your life can be more satisfying; and what cannot be changed—it might be well to consider these truths as guidelines. You will find that they apply to almost all of life's situations. And sometimes a sensible guideline is all we need to keep our lives on an even keel.

We mentioned in an earlier chapter that we all are composed of at least three main spheres: the spiritual; the intellectual and the creative—our mind; and the physical. The combination of all these traits is what makes each of us like no one else on earth. We all have some things in common with many people—some of whom we know and some of whom we don't know—but there is no one anywhere exactly like us in every detail.

Women are often ambivalent about what they want to do with their lives—sometimes it's hard to find the energy, psychic and physical, to change. When the three elements that make up any human being are in harmony, then we feel contented, energetic, positive, self-confident. When the spiritual, intellectual, the physical, are in synch, then we can move forward with our lives. We can do more, plan more, care more. *Be* more.

The Spiritual You

What do you mean when you think of the spiritual? A religious experience? Visiting a house of worship? It could be, partly. But we think that the all-encompassing, fundamental meaning of "spiritual" refers to everything that you are in your heart. Are you good? Are you reliable? Are you honest? Do you help others? Do you love others? Most important, do you love yourself?

We think this last question—do you love yourself?—is at the bottom of all the other questions. When women have confidence in themselves, strong egos, self-esteem, when they decide to make a difference in their *own* lives, that's when things really explode, when great things are accomplished.

If you can make a difference in your own life, you automatically make a difference in your family's life—

your spouse, your children, your parents, anyone you come in contact with. When women are confident, and getting better all the time, and making their lives happier and more successful, that's when they turn their attention outward and help not only those whom they know but also those whom they don't know who need help. When women have self-esteem, they're strong. That's when they share their own success, and when they give to others.

Is it hard to believe that so much would get better because you get your life in order? And help to establish financial security for your family? And open your own dry cleaning store and employ two other people? And because you're happy, you're a joy to your family and friends? That's improving the quality of your life, through your own efforts. And what if millions of other women in this country were able to do just that? A great deal *would* be accomplished. You first help yourself, then you help others. You do unto others . . .

Laura Balverde-Sanchez, one of our 1988 Women of Enterprise Awards winners, is president of the New El Rey Sausage Company, in Vernon, California. This thirty-nine-year-old entrepreneur enjoys being a role model for other women who are trying to make their way in the business world: "As a woman who just happens to be Hispanic, I can help motivate women to reach for the stars and take a chance as I did," she says. Also, she believes that through her business she can take "personal social responsibility for improving the state of women and Hispanics."

Laura Balverde-Sanchez was born in California to parents of Mexican ancestry—they were not rich, but very hard-working. Balverde-Sanchez grew up amidst a strong work ethic and the belief that she could do anything she wanted.

As a very small child, Balverde-Sanchez entered the business world with enthusiasm: hers was not just any ordinary lemonade stand. She boosted her sales by also selling avocados, a favorite in her Hispanic neighborhood. In time, she worked her way through college, married, and continued working hard.

In 1983, Balverde-Sanchez and her husband mortgaged all their assets to purchase the El Rey Sausage Company, which was on the brink of bankruptcy. The couple was faced with a daunting task. El Rey's reputation was shaky—their delivery and service had become unreliable—and Balverde-Sanchez found out that she had a lot to learn about the meat business—and about a balance sheet. Anxious to learn, she begged her accountant: "Show me which numbers have to go up and which ones should come down."

She learned about those numbers, and also about marketing. She had to salvage the reputation of her company. With the help of her husband, Balverde-Sanchez convinced some small grocers to carry her products, which gave her the courage to approach the larger accounts, like Safeway. Today, the company produces four kinds of sausage, as well as other Hispanic-style foods. El Rey's products are now sold in twelve states, and there are plans for national distribution.

Balverde-Sanchez never forgets that she is a role model in her community—and she gives back to that community. She knows that others can follow her example. For ten years, she taught courses in citizenship as well as English as a second language; she has served on the board of directors of the Hispanic

Women's Council, and is a member of Comision Femenil, a nonprofit service organization.

Another 1988 Women of Enterprise Awards winner, Charito Kruvant, has a lot in common with Laura Balverde-Sanchez. To Charito Kruvant, effecting social change is one of the guiding forces in her life. And as the president of Creative Associates International, a management consulting firm in Washington, D.C., Kruvant is often in a position to help others—educating minority children being a top priority.

Charito Kruvant, like so many of our Women of Enterprise winners, has had to overcome problems that could defeat a woman less willing to fight for what she wanted. Kruvant is dyslexic—dyslexia is a serious learning disability that makes reading and writing very difficult without special training. In addition, she knows the problems of being an outsider, a child forced from her home.

Kruvant has indeed come a long way to reach success in Washington, D.C. She was born in the mountains of Bolivia; her parents of Indian ancestry. When Kruvant was eight years old, her family was caught up in a military revolution and forced to escape to Argentina, where Charito Kruvant's dark skin marked her as an outsider and her dyslexia at first made making her way in school very difficult.

But Charito Kruvant adjusted: she was very intelligent, and her good memory enabled her to succeed in her lessons. She was also an excellent athlete and she "learned early that if I worked harder than everybody else, I could be part of the group." Indeed, she did well, and won the opportunity to attend high school in South Orange, New Jersey, as a foreign exchange student. Eventually, she earned a liberal arts degree in Argentina and returned to the United States to study for a teacher's license. Trying to give to the community, she tutored inner-city kids in Newark: "This was my first exposure to the universality of poverty," says Kruvant. "I had a vision of America as an affluent country. Suddenly, I realized that poor kids are poor kids."

In 1968, Charito Kruvant, now married to an American, moved to Washington, D.C., where she created educational programs for minority children. She became familiar with the inner workings of government and bureaucracy and gained in confidence. She now trusted her own abilities to lead others and to develop projects of different sorts.

Creative Associates International started in Kruvant's basement in 1977. Its list of services included management training, human resources development, and marketing strategies for government as well as the private sector. Over the years, the company has grown to seventy-five full-time employees, with annual revenues exceeding $6 million.

For all her accomplishments, Charito Kruvant has never stepped back from what she considers her responsibility in helping others, both children and minority adults, and today is focusing efforts on the development of minority women business owners. She cannot be sure in what future directions her energies might lead her, but today Charito Kruvant says, "I will never let go of my dreams because they eventually become realities." Clearly, Kruvant is a wonderful role model for all women.

The two Women of Enterprise mentioned above have taken time out from the building of successful enterprises to help others. They have done it through their businesses, in hiring people who needed jobs, but they have also donated time and energy to helping various organizations. We should not forget that there are thousands of organizations in this country and in your community that need your interest, your time, and your money.

Helping others is an element in your spiritual growth. It's part of the golden rule that we talked about earlier. You help others when you can—you may need help yourself someday.

You can help people in countless ways. You can hire them. You can train those who would be unemployable. Or you can volunteer your time and attention to any one of a thousand worthwhile organizations. Especially if you fit into the entrepreneurial category, you can usually find at least a few hours to give away to your fellow human beings—or to endangered animals, or to developer-targeted buildings that should be preserved, or to threatened wetlands. . . . Whatever interests you.

Why do you want to? Especially if you're not going to be making any money. If you do get involved, you will probably find that you are paid in other ways. Eleanor Raynolds, a partner in the executive search firm of Ward Howell International, is the co-author with her husband, John Raynolds, of *Beyond Success: How Volunteer Service Can Help You Begin Making a Life Instead of Just a Living*. Raynolds says: "Service can illuminate a new path, a new direction for your life. It makes you less self-conscious, and in the process parts of yourself emerge that you may have unintentionally kept submerged. . . . Service is personally liberating. It helps to break the constricting cycle of self-absorption. . . . Service gives us a sense, if not exactly of control, at least of responsible participation in the affairs of the surrounding world."

Volunteering can only help you grow. You lose time, but the return is worth more. Some additional benefits that you may not have thought of:

▽ As you get involved with others, your own troubles become less. A lot of people have it very hard—perhaps you will gain new perspective.

▽ You can have fun. Particularly if you're working hard to get a new business off the ground, you may find a break relaxing. Do you love animals? Spend a few hours a week at a pet adoption center. Or work with a program that brings animals to visit retirement homes.

▽ You can use skills that no job has ever demanded of you. Do you love to draw? Find an after-school program for inner-city kids and fingerpaint with the youngest children. It will be therapeutic for you as well, and you can become an art teacher for a few afternoons a week.

▽ A volunteer job can be an education in itself. You can work for an organization that does something that you know nothing about. Do you love kids but know very little about handicaps of various kinds? It might be enlightening for you to become an aide at a school for children who are severely learning disabled.

▽ You meet people with interests similar to yours. As you work together, you will get to know these people well. You may gain a new friend, a spouse, a client.

▽ You can gain in confidence and organizational ability. Many helping organizations are run like businesses. As people get to know you, and you achieve positions of trust, you may have to speak to groups, write reports, chair meetings.

But we think it's the intangible rewards that you will find most satisfying if you can manage to join with others to help in your community. It always seems as if it's the busiest people who have the time to devote to others. They also have time to be successful, and creative, and fulfilled. Perhaps you could join that group.

The Intellectual You

The intellectual aspect of what makes you unique is the use you make of your mind as you interact with the world around you—what you've learned, what you've created, how you measure up to the competition and to the standards that you've set for yourself.

The confidence that you have in your own intellectual abilities, which are the tools that you have to manage your life, has a lot to do with the face that you present to the world at large. If you have that inner confidence, then you will appear confident to those around you. If you have a poor opinion of yourself and don't really think that you are in control of your own destiny, this is going to be immediately apparent to those you meet.

But you probably know all this. If you lack in self-esteem, this no doubt has been true since you were quite young. You know the feeling of not being in control, but just reacting to events around you. We hope the histories of our Women of Enterprise winners have illustrated a few truths that you may never have recognized.

1. Everyone is scared sometimes. You are not alone in feeling insecure, inadequate, untrained. Every one of the Women of Enterprise had to start at a beginning, all by herself. Success for each of these women was gradual. Confidence was mostly self-taught, and the result of trial and error. They were each willing to fail, and then try again for success. Not one started out with any sure knowledge that success was a sure thing. The confidence they felt was not in their endeavors, whatever they were, but in their ability to overcome trial and trouble.

2. You *will* learn by doing. You have to make your plans as best you can, and then jump in. No one can predict what will happen. But you will probably be able to figure a way around any difficulty. And you will gradually learn the ins and outs of your enterprise.

And having said that, please be warned: no new venture is certain, whether it's a franchise, a shop, a service. DO NOT RISK THE LIFE SAVINGS OF YOUR ENTIRE EXTENDED FAMILY. Truly, there is always another way. Do not mortgage your parents' home, or sell your family's most precious heirloom. Do not take out a bank loan that you will never be able to repay if the business fails. You won't forgive yourself if you "borrow" from your children's college fund, or decide to drop your health insurance because you need the cash.

In other words, figure out exactly how much you stand to lose if the enterprise goes belly up, and the only things left are some dead fish floating on the surface of the pond. If those dead carp are now the sum total of your fortune, this was a bad investment.

3. You are rarely completely alone in any new venture. You may have become a sales representative, in which case you have the guidance of the company whose products you're selling; you may have a supportive spouse, parents, friends—any of whom might lend a hand or money if times get tight. You might have business partners, or even a talented employee to soothe you when you panic. Sometimes customers are supportive and helpful, sometimes suppliers. You never know from what avenue help might arrive—it's your job to be hardworking, and well organized, and optimistic, and confident. There is no point in not hoping for the best—sometimes it happens that way.

4. In time, you will gain confidence. You will also gain stature in your chosen field. Step by step, you learn your trade, you meet people, they learn you are reliable, they become clients. As clients, they will like your product and order more. You will meet the payroll, and maybe have a few new ideas. These ideas may be successful, and you will be proud. This is a good kind of pride, the kind that's a synonym for confidence. And it's this kind of confidence that ena-

bles a woman to trust in the results of her own hard work and good ideas. Once she trusts herself, then she is no longer afraid to take another step.

5. If you persevere, eventually you will literally become a new person. As strength builds on strength, and you learn to cope with failure, your character will form. You will react to situations in ways you never would have thought of, or thought possible, when you were starting your new venture. It's a way of growing up, but also of growing better.

We're very admiring of the perseverance of a 1989 Women of Enterprise Awards winner, Charlotte Brannstrom, president of Greater Flint Temporaries, a temporary-help agency in Flint, Michigan. When it came time to spread her wings, she was scared, but she stuck with it. And it *was* frightening. Says Brannstrom: "Twelve years ago I decided to start my own business because my boss refused to give me a twenty-five-dollar raise. Her reaction to me was, 'What are you complaining about, Charlotte, you make damn good money for a woman.' That made me mad.

"I had to do something to gain control over my business life. It was a big step for me and I was scared. In fact, I was downright terrified. But once I overcame that fear and made up my mind that I was going to go ahead and do it, I didn't look back. I'm not saying it was easy. Sometimes it was very difficult to continue on. But every step has been worth it. Running my own business has been satisfying and extremely rewarding."

It was thirteen years ago that Charlotte Brannstrom's boss refused to give her that twenty-five-dollar raise. When she bravely set out to open her temporary-help agency, she had no college degree or financial backing. Brannstrom came from New York City, one of ten children born to poor parents, both alcoholics. The story of her early years tells of foster care, and child abuse, and not enough to eat.

Adulthood brought little relief. Her new business got off to a shaky start in 1977, and for years was buffeted by Flint's periodic economic recessions; her mother-in-law was killed in an automobile accident, and in 1982 she lost her oldest daughter in yet another crash. Brannstrom's twenty-one-year marriage had failed, but she continued to build up her business throughout all the years of personal anguish. She prevailed, kept her equilibrium, and built a successful company with annual revenues approaching $2 million. Charlotte Brannstrom believes strongly in personal growth, and has a gritty determination to become better: "You have to forget where you've been and concentrate on where you're going," she advises. She's a role model "for people who are enduring and overcoming great personal crises while functioning in the real world. I'd like to show others how."

The Avon Report

At Avon, we like to know what women entrepreneurs think about their lives, and their jobs, and their hopes for the future. We need to know how the women of America tick if we are to continue to serve them effectively—they are, after all, both our sales representatives and our customers. Or potential sales representatives and customers. We need to know how things change for women, and how they remain the same. And how they *should* change.

Many women each year apply for our Women of Enterprise Awards. For the three-year period 1987–1989, 450 of these applicants—all successful women entrepreneurs—completed an in-depth questionnaire for us, answering questions about their businesses, giving vital statistics, and telling us a little about themselves. For example, one of our questions asked, "When others said it couldn't be done, you did it. Please tell us how and at what point you said to yourself, 'I've made it!' "

We thought the answers would be of interest, and inspiration, to other women who were attempting their own entrepreneurial ventures—it's always invigorating to hear about those who have gone before, and been successful. The survey was conducted for us by New World Decisions, an opinion research firm, which also analyzed the answers. The results appear in the publication *The Avon Report: A National Attitude Survey on Successful Women Entrepreneurs.*

What did we learn that might be of use to you? "*The Avon Report* shows that women entrepreneurs may choose different paths to success, yet each path can lead to a profitable enterprise," suggests Marilyn Frasier Pollock, Ph.D., an anthropologist and expert on women's entrepreneurship who is co-owner of New World Decisions. Dr. Pollock continues: "In fact, successful women entrepreneurs who pursue goals *other* than sales growth or profit are found slightly more often at the highest level of annual growth sales—$500,000 and above." So motivation can be something other than a dollar chase—it could be a need for self-fulfillment or a desire to help others. None of it precludes success.

We'll share with you some of the questions in the report—and the responses. Perhaps you can get some idea of the wide range of needs, goals, ambitions that exist among this nation's women entrepreneurs—as well as the fears and obstacles that they had to overcome.

WHAT FACTORS MOTIVATED YOU TO START A BUSINESS?

The main motivation, we found, was a strong desire for a greater sense of control over their careers. These women wanted flexibility. There was more positive "pull" rather than negative "push." Strong desire to change was more prevalent than job loss, family crisis, or personal tragedy.

WERE YOU INSPIRED BY A ROLE MODEL?

Seven in ten said yes. That role model was usually someone quite close to the respondent: a parent (35 percent), a spouse (20 percent), or a relative or friend (20 percent).

WHAT IS YOUR PERSONAL DEFINITION OF SUCCESS?

Almost 38 percent described success as happiness or self-fulfillment. One owner of an insurance agency wrote that success is "to be truly happy and satisfied by your work. We spend the better part of our days at work. We've got to love what we do!"

Thirty percent talked about the challenge of entrepreneurship and the satisfaction that comes with achievement, and 20 percent said that success was achieved through helping people. The owner of a talent counseling business told us, "You have achieved success in your life when you can reach out to help others attain it."

A very small minority—a little more than 12 percent—described success as measured by revenues and profits.

WHAT IS THE SINGLE MOST IMPORTANT QUALITY THAT LED TO YOUR SUCCESS?

The overwhelming majority (77 percent) talk about an "internal perspective," meaning a healthy or optimistic attitude or a passion for perseverance. Included within this category would be such traits as self-confidence and a sense of humor. Only 23 percent attributed business success to their management skills, creativity, goal setting, ability to communicate—the "external perspective."

Both perspectives are important, but it is clear that business success depends on much more than the ability to read a balance sheet. It depends on humanistic skills of caring, flexibility and an ability to adapt, and an up-beat approach to life.

WHAT WAS THE MAJOR PROFESSIONAL OBSTACLE YOU FACED IN FORMING YOUR BUSINESS?

The answer to this was not a lack of business skills but rather convincing the business world of their ability. The respondents did not believe that a real lack of business skills stood in their way, although lack of expertise about the *specific* type of business that they might have launched was a problem for 14 percent.

A full one-third emphasized the feeling of being an outsider in the business world—men especially did not accept them as equal or credit their competence as entrepreneurs. These women cited as their greatest obstacle being a woman in a nontraditional field— think back to our Women of Enterprise winners who are in heavy construction—and not being taken seriously.

When asked how they overcame professional obstacles, the answers were the same: hard work, determination, and networking with colleagues—a little help from their friends.

WHAT WAS YOUR MAJOR PERSONAL OBSTACLE?

The largest group—40 percent—cited low self-esteem. Other common problems: lack of support from family and friends, difficulties in balancing family and work.

And how did they overcome these problems? The respondents describe four major ways:

1. Support from family, friends, colleagues (51 percent). This shows that everyone's experience is

different. Some entrepreneurs clearly get a great deal of support from family and friends—yet it's a problem for others.

2. Psychological and spiritual growth (39 percent). Adversity and life's changes do seem to spur personal growth in some women. Increased self-esteem and confidence are the by-products of this kind of inner growth.

3. Hard work (28 percent). No matter what field you go into, this is bottom line. Be prepared.

4. Networking (11 percent). You can make use—in a dignified, professional way, of course—of anyone you've ever met who might be able to help you. You know ex-co-workers, ex-bosses, friends of your spouse, parents of your children's friends, that nice woman in the post office, your parents, their friends, your entire class in high school, the people who are in your pottery class, the teacher of your pottery class, your dentist, accountant, their wives and mothers. And then there are all those people out there whom you haven't met yet.

There are certain rules of behavior. Be clear about what sort of information you need, do not waste their time, and be grateful for any lead. A thank-you note for a favor is *always* necessary, perhaps a nice box of peaches if someone has gone above and beyond to help you out. The old saw that we heard from our mothers—"Put on some makeup and comb your hair even if you're just going to the supermarket. You never know whom you'll meet"—is good advice. You never do know from what avenue a lead, a client, a new idea will arrive.

WOULD YOU DO ANYTHING DIFFERENTLY IF YOU COULD START ALL OVER AGAIN?

Nineteen percent said no, they wouldn't change a thing; 11 percent would plan growth more carefully, 10 percent would try to invest more capital, 7 percent would learn more about marketing—but there was no overwhelming lack that any of our respondents felt. Nothing major to warn you about.

WHICH TWO PROFESSIONAL SKILLS ARE MOST ESSENTIAL TO SUCCESS?

Not surprisingly, good management skills were ranked highest by our respondents (24 percent); good marketing skills came in second (13 percent). Also important: solid work experience, relationships with professional advisers, networking, and a good business plan.

WHICH TWO PERSONAL SKILLS ARE MOST ESSENTIAL TO SUCCESS?

Tying for first place are high self-esteem and self-confidence (23 percent) and honesty and integrity (23 percent). It seems to us that if women can make use of good self-confidence to become successful, then they can put that honesty and integrity to work and perhaps put a more human face on economic life in this country. None of these traits preclude good, hard-headed business sense and ambition.

Can you identify with some of these respondents? These are women who have already made it in the business world. They're really women who are just like you. All you need to do is focus some of your energy, and realize that what they say is accurate: you can do anything with a little self-confidence and a lot of hard work. These, and the knowledge that success is possible, seem to have helped many of our respondents' dreams to come true.

The Physical You

In order for you to achieve *your* dreams, you need certain tools to help you. We've talked about self-esteem, and confidence, and business plans, and networking, and helping others. Yes, this is all important, but there is an area that is even more basic than your spiritual life, your creativity, your plans for the future.

You have to be physically able to bring your dreams to life—you need a healthy, vigorous, articulate, attractive package to present to the outside world. You need the energy to think clearly and move energetically through your day. You need a healthy body that will not fail you in times of stress. Your business as well as your personal life depends on others' opinion of you. There is absolutely no point in driving people away when you can be as attractive as the competition.

And what of your own self-esteem? When you look in the mirror, what do you see? An attractive, confident, neatly dressed woman with the kind of energy that is a magnet to anyone who might cross your path? If not, do not despair. We can help you. The next chapters will be devoted to the inner and outer you—the physical you, how you feel, how you look, what improvements you might want to make.

It's not true that beauty is only skin deep. What's on the surface frequently tells the world about your state of mind, your opinion of yourself, your inner strength, your self-discipline. You can learn to show the world that you're a winner—and you can learn to believe it yourself.

7

THE BASICS: HEALTH . . . NUTRITION . . . EXERCISE

H

ow you are inside—your personality and character—is mostly the result of what's happened to you in life up to now, and how you've handled it. How you are outside—your style, vitality, apparent health—is partly due to genetic inheritance, but mostly the result of what you've decided to do with it.

There are some things in life that cannot be ignored. The way you look, and the way you feel, are two of those things. How you look affects the way other people react to you. People respond positively when they meet an attractive woman. This doesn't necessarily mean pretty or glamorous. It means well-groomed, energetic, appropriately dressed. You have chosen the image that you present to the outside world. It says immediately to those you meet: "This woman is in control of her life."

And they are right. Every woman likes to have options. When you make choices about how you look, and are pleased with the result because it's right for *you,* you're not only pleasing those around you, you're sending a positive message to yourself.

How you feel depends both on your health and on your state of mind. If your health is good, and your outlook positive, the result is a vitality and optimism that enable women to try for new goals and achieve them.

Some women are blessed with good health and energy without having to do very much about it. They can eat anything and not gain weight. They don't exercise and their muscle tone remains firm. They are never sick.

These women are very rare. Most of you have to pay careful attention to everything that goes into making your physical self the best it can be. You'll find that if you incorporate a health and fitness regime into your life, and make it part of your day-to-day routine, in time you will feel better, and look better, and have the energy to sculpt your life into the shape that you want.

A Healthy Body

How do you know if you are in good health? First, listen to your body. If all is not right, it will probably tell you, loud and clear. See your doctor if you notice the following:

    ▽ Low energy level that never seems to improve
    ▽ Racing pulse or heart palpitations
    ▽ Headaches
    ▽ Dizziness, blurred vision

▽ Persistent pain *anywhere*
▽ Unexplained bleeding
▽ Aching muscles or joints
▽ Weakness in the muscles
▽ Change in your menstrual cycle
▽ Hair, skin, and nails that seem subnormal

These symptoms might mean nothing at all. They could be caused by a diet that's wrong for you nutritionally, or lack of exercise, or too much stress. But it should not be up to you to decide what, if anything, is wrong. This is the time to call in the experts, your team of medical advisers.

People looking for medical help usually ask their friends and family for referrals. Or you can request a list at your local hospital or medical association. These places will not recommend just one physician; it's unethical. Typically, you will get three or four names in each specialty.

Although there are more women physicians than there used to be, the chances are that most of the recommended names will be men. If you think that you would feel more comfortable with a woman doctor, persevere. You will find one. They're out there.

Not every illness has symptoms that you would notice yourself. And prevention is the best possible medicine. Make up your mind that there are some doctors whom you should see on a regular basis. Every woman should know:

1. A general practitioner. The old-time family physician is hard to find. It's an internist that you're looking for—the person who will give you a yearly

checkup and treat you for a cold. If you have specific complaints, the GP might recommend that you see a specialist and will furnish you with a name.

2. A gynecologist. You must see this person once a year for an exam and a Pap smear. You should make more frequent appointments if you have a history of gynecological trouble or if you are taking birth control pills. Your gynecologist will advise you about mammography—a low-dosage X ray of the breast that often discovers tumors before they're big enough to feel.

3. An ophthalmologist. This is your eye doctor, who will see if your vision has changed and also will check for glaucoma and possible tumors. If you have headaches, this is the checkup you should have first. A visit every couple of years is probably enough if you have no problems.

4. A dentist. This health practitioner will suggest how often you should come. If you have no special difficulties, a visit every six months for a thorough cleaning will do.

5. A specialist. You may be among those women who are physically challenged. This could be a serious problem that affects the way you live your life—you're confined to a wheelchair, for example. Or it might be relatively minor—you're a mild diabetic who must stay on a rigid diet but does not need insulin. You will be under the care of a physician who specializes in your problem.

HOW TO CHOOSE A DOCTOR

Your internist has retired and you've gotten three new names from friends. How do you choose among them?

Here are some guidelines that you can follow in most situations when looking for a doctor.

▽ You can ask for an appointment just to talk. You will have to pay for it, but this is money well spent. You want to meet this person before an emergency arises. If the doctor refuses, this is not the person for you.

▽ You are interviewing the doctor, not the other way around. Does this person seem to mind answering questions about fees? About the relationship between patient and physician? About medical ethics?

▽ Does this doctor have a good educational background? The best doctors don't necessarily come from the best medical schools, but there are some medical diploma mills in other countries that probably are not adequate. Board certification in a specialty is a plus—it shows additional training.

▽ Are the physician's office hours convenient for you? And the office itself? Can you get to it easily? And does this doctor have backup in case he or she is ill or on vacation?

▽ Most important: Do you like this person? If you do not, find someone else. Your doctor is a partner in keeping you healthy and fit. You want someone you feel comfortable with. And the choice is completely up to you.

A Healthy Attitude

The power of positive thinking is a real concept. It works. In the April 1989 issue, *Working Woman* talked about the "take-charge approach to staying healthy . . . a whole new area of science, known as psychoneuroimmunology."

All this means is that researchers are finally taking a scientific look at what a great many people have known for a long time: the way we think has a lot to do with the way we feel. And our frame of mind seems to influence our general health and resilience in times of stress.

It's much too soon to say for sure that reduction of stress prevents ulcers, or heart attacks, or cancer, but studies are beginning to show that women who believe that they have control over their lives, and react to stressful situations in positive, problem-solving ways, are healthier and happier.

Some great stress reducers:

1. Learn relaxation techniques. There are books, tapes, and classes available everywhere. You can become expert in controlling anxious thoughts and smoothing tense muscles. Biofeedback is one technique that has proved helpful.

2. Exercise. When you work out, your body releases chemicals in the brain called endorphins. These are a natural tranquilizer.

3. Get lots of rest. Nothing makes cares disappear more than a good night's sleep. If you have trouble sleeping, stay away from pills. Try a warm glass of milk.

Yes, it works. Dairy products contain the sleep inducer tryptophan.

4. Laugh. When you laugh, the level of those endorphins rises. And if you can treat your problems with a sense of humor, you won't lose perspective.

5. Make lists of the good things in your life. In other words, count your blessings.

6. Get a pet. Pet owners seem to have fewer heart attacks and strokes. It is good for you to take care of another living being. You won't concentrate so much on your own troubles.

7. Keep your support network of friends and family alive. People who care for you want to help. But you have to let them know when it's necessary.

8. Try something new. Learn a foreign language or how to build a harpsichord. Stretch yourself. Be creative.

9. Don't be a victim. If you find yourself in a sticky situation, act. Don't let yourself be pushed around. It's very damaging to self-esteem. There is nothing more stressful than waiting for something unpleasant to develop. If you can, *you* make things happen.

10. Finally, remember the power of positive thinking. Don't expect the worst. Expect the best. It can happen just as easily.

You Really Are What You Eat

American women usually associate the word "diet" with weight loss. We are preoccupied with being thin, and sometimes pay obsessive attention to what we eat.

Think of all the books and magazine articles that have been written about weight loss. Over the years, we have been exposed to the grapefruit diet, low-carbohydrate, high-protein, Pritikin, Weight Watchers, Scarsdale, brown rice, liquid . . .

The result of these diets is often the same: initial weight loss, then gradual weight gain until the old levels are reached. It has been proved again and again that the only way to take off unwanted pounds and keep them off is to eliminate unhealthy eating habits and learn to love, or at least to live with, a lifetime regime of sensible eating. Exercise to accompany good eating patterns is a must.

Of course, not all American women need to lose weight, or want to. Some women are too thin. Some might be a little overweight but feel more comfortable that way. If they are in good health, and happy with themselves, that's the most important thing. It's a mistake to buy into the concept of the ideal woman that the media are selling us through TV ads, magazines, and films. We should be sophisticated enough, with sufficient self-confidence in our own opinion, to decide for ourselves how we want to look. It's important that we please ourselves first. Only if we are dissatisfied is there any pressing reason to change.

If several years have gone by, and your weight has gone up and down like a yo-yo, and you've tried all kinds of diets and can't stick to them, it's time to try a professional. Talk with your doctor, or a nutritionist, and get a program tailor-made for you. Reward yourself for every few pounds lost. If you are successful, you will collect huge dividends in renewed self-confidence and pride in your ability to see a project through to the end.

The word "diet" means more than weight loss. It includes all the food and drink that we consume. If we listened to what our bodies are telling us every day, we would eat only those foods that are good for us, and would find in the process that we had no problems with weight gain or loss. Our systems would be in balance, and we would weigh what is right for us.

But we don't all listen to our bodies. We all know women who like nothing better than a lettuce and cucumber salad for lunch—they really enjoy the crunch, and the combination of flavors, and the feeling that good things are going into their bodies.

But what if you really crave a fast-food burger just dripping with fat and ketchup, which is loaded with sugar, on a bun that has the nutritional content of cardboard? Or you're a chocoholic and your idea of heaven is a chocolate-covered anything? All is not lost—you can have these treats . . . every once in a while.

We all know that life is not easy. There are many areas in *your* life in which you have to exercise discipline, and self-control, for a greater good. Constant self-indulgence will not produce good results anywhere—on the job, in your relationship with your spouse, in disciplining your children. That's the thing about being an adult. You exercise adult-strength self-discipline for adult-strength rewards.

In this case, if you establish a lifelong routine of good eating habits and exercise, you will be rewarded with energy, the self-confidence that comes from deciding to do something and then doing it, and a body that can fulfill the demands that you place upon it. What's the point of going through life at half-speed? Your physical being is the machine that's going to get you there with the throttle open wide.

Remember Those Food Groups?

A diet that is well balanced will keep your body healthy and your mind healthy . . . and you will attain your ideal weight as a bonus. But good eating habits have to be planned for. One of the reasons that American women overeat is that they think they don't have the time to eat healthy foods—it's so much quicker to stop at a fast-food restaurant for something nonnutritious like donuts and coffee.

You *do* have time to establish a routine. With practice, it will become second nature to you. Plan your meals and snacks in advance, bring food with you—to the office, for example—if necessary, and establish a healthful routine. You can be in control of your own eating habits. You will find it easier if you schedule carefully and plan ahead. *No one* needs to fill up habitually on junk foods.

A REMINDER: COUNT CALORIES

It is sometimes hard to eat properly. It takes determination and knowledge of what's good for you. It is *not* hard to figure out how much to eat. You just have to count calories. Pay attention to the calorie content of the food you eat.

The word "calorie" signifies the amount of energy that is released as heat when the food you eat is metabolized by your body, which needs a certain number of calories to function. If you take in too many, they are stored as fat. Too few, and you lose weight.

To figure out how many you need to maintain your weight without gaining or losing, try the following computations.

If you are moderately active: Multiply your weight by 15. That is the number of calories you need to maintain your energy during a day. Do you weigh 110? Then you need to take in 1,650 calories.

If you are very active: Add 200 to the above figure. You will need 1,850 to maintain your weight of 110.

If you are sedentary: Subtract 200 from the calculations for a moderately active woman. If you weigh 110, you need 1,450 calories to stay at 110.

If you want to gain, you will take in more calories than you need; if you want to lose, take in fewer.

Information about good diet can be found in every newspaper and magazine in all parts of this country. TV programs talk about what we should eat, and why. Sometimes it seems that if we pay attention to everything we hear, we would never eat anything. Red meat is lethal because it can raise cholesterol, fish is full of mercury. Our fresh fruits and vegetables are sprayed with poisons, and dairy products full of terrible chemicals consumed by the cows. People who eat yogurt every day may face glaucoma down the road. Some of these warnings are true, and some exaggerated. The worst cases are being investigated by government agencies, which have the power to impose controls.

Your best bet is to practice moderation. A good balance of foods is the basis of the most sensible kind of diet. Those pie charts that we all memorized in the fifth grade that talked about the basic food groups had a lot going for them. We *all* need to eat foods rich in protein, fiber, carbohydrates, fats, vitamins, and minerals. All those old nutrition rules still apply. There is no substitute for a varied diet of wholesome, fresh foods.

And think of your children. Whatever you eat is sending a strong message to them about acceptable eating habits. If you gorge on potato chips when you're all watching TV, what do you think they'll buy when they're on their own? Have a big bowl of butter-free popcorn on hand instead. Kids really like yogurt, and carrot sticks, and low-fat cheeses if they're introduced to them early with your enthusiastic endorsement.

You can't go wrong if you include the following in your diet:

▽ Anything fresh. Fresh fruits and vegetables in season have the most vitamins and minerals. But buy fresh-frozen out of season. The frozen fruits and vegetables are in reality much closer to fresh than those tired peppers that have been traveling from South America for weeks.

▽ All those foods that furnish us with the whole spectrum of vitamins and minerals that we need daily yet are not loaded with fats and sugars: low-fat dairy products, fruits and vegetables of all kinds, fish, eggs, whole-grain breads, pasta and rice, some organ meats like liver, nuts, wheat germ, poultry, honey as a sweetener (because it's so sweet, you need much less of it than you would cane or beet sugar).

There's nothing wrong with a vitamin supplement, especially if your doctor prescribes it, but be careful of overdoses. Some vitamins are not excreted automatically if you've taken too much. The ones to be especially careful of are vitamins A and D.

∇ Foods rich in fiber seem to cut down on cancer of the colon and are frequently vitamin rich. Try: bran cereals, corn, beans, broccoli, potatoes with the skin, Brussels sprouts, apples, peaches, cabbage, peas, strawberries.

∇ Fruit drinks instead of sodas and other sweet drinks. Use your blender to combine crushed fresh fruit with orange or pineapple juice. Your kids will love it.

∇ Lots of water. The average adult body contains about forty-five quarts of water and loses about three quarts a day. These have to be replaced if the body is to function properly.

Try to avoid:

∇ Alcohol. It's fattening and not nutritious.

∇ Caffeine-loaded drinks. Try herbal or fruit-flavored teas.

∇ Anything fried. You can usually prepare the same food using no fat, or very little. The vegetable sprays are good because they cut way down on the amount of oil used.

▽ Sugar. Gives a quick high, but then the level of blood sugar sinks rapidly, which causes fatigue and sometimes depression. It's fun occasionally—you want to taste your child's birthday cake—but try to go easy on sugary sweets.

▽ Processed food of all kinds. This could be anything from frozen diet dinners (which have amazing amounts of sodium in them) to canned baked beans (lots of sugar). Get in the habit of cooking with your family. You will have fun and your diet will improve enormously.

Learn to Love Those Workout Tapes

Exercise, like following the correct diet, takes discipline and concentration. But if you want good muscle tone, and a sleek line that shows your clothes off properly, as well as energy and bouncy good health, you *have* to follow some sort of program. You want your heart to pump energetically, and your lungs to expand, and your muscles to get a workout.

How you go about this is up to you. Each woman has different needs and a schedule peculiar to her own life. The idea is not necessarily to work out until you look like Jane Fonda, or Cheryl Tiegs, or Cher. You want to reach your own optimum energy level, your own level of fitness.

Sharlyne R. Powell, one of our 1987 Women of Enterprise winners, is an excellent example of a woman who found her own niche in the competitive world of fitness as a business. In 1983, she launched Women At Large Systems, the country's first fitness program for large women. To succeed, says Powell, you have to "work hard, hire a good support team, and proceed with sheer guts."

Powell, herself a large woman, had found herself depressed when she got no results from any of the several exercise programs that she'd tried. She says, "I couldn't keep up with the routines. I was embarrassed and humiliated, self-esteem battered." With no previous experience, she experimented with a new kind of low-impact aerobics system specially tailored for larger women.

At first, she received very little support from health and fitness professionals: the word was that large women were health risks and, in addition, just didn't want to exercise.

Sharlyne Powell knew better and continued with her experiment. She completed her exercise program and hired a board of directors. She was ready for business.

Then she made a mistake. Powell hired the same sort of fitness instructors that most clients were used to seeing in other salons: women who were not only fit but thin. Powell's target clientele of larger women were alienated from the very first. But Powell recognized her error almost immediately, and she and her partner filled in as instructors until they could train a staff of larger women.

Business has been great ever since. Powell's company is now franchised in both the United States and Canada, and she has released a home workout video as well as designed a line of exercise clothing. Powell knows what it's like to feel less than confident, and her clients may attend workshops in hair design, makeup, fashion, as well as support groups aimed at raising self-esteem.

The lesson to be learned from Sharlyne Powell's experience is that although you do need some sort of exercise program, it should be tailored to fit your schedule, and your needs. You may be too busy to go to a health club on a regular basis. Or too easily bored to use an exercise bicycle at home alone.

You have endless choices, limited only by your imagination. The one requirement is that you choose something and then stick to it—exercising energetically at least three hours during the course of a week, more if possible. That's less than thirty minutes a day. Not only will you benefit by increasing your stamina, and improving your muscle tone and body line, but you will gain in the confidence that comes from planning and completing any project.

Some possibilities:

▽ Jog. This is especially fun if you do it with a friend. It requires minimal investment—a good pair of running shoes is all you need. Be careful not to overdo it, particularly when you first start up. New studies show that jogging too strenuously can strain the heart a well as damage bones and ligaments in legs and feet.

▽ Walk. Start the day with a brisk walk. Opt for walking in lieu of riding whenever you have the chance, particularly if you have to go a mile or less.

▽ Exercise during the day. Do isometrics or low-impact aerobics whenever you have a free moment or in downtime between appointments.

▽ Skip rope. This is another very inexpensive way to stay fit. It may even bring back fond memories of your childhood.

▽ Swim. Take advantage of indoor pools in your area for year-round swimming. If you don't know how to swim, take lessons. It's always good to at least be able to float.

▽ Lift weights. If this appeals to you, ask a friend with know-how or a trainer for advice on what's right for you.

▽ Exercise on your own. Buy one of the videos on the market. Concentrate on strengthening a weak part of your body. Your doctor can give you a list of appropriate exercises.

▽ Bicyle. There are bicycle clubs all over. Or just do it on your own. It's great exercise and a good way to meet people.

▽ Play team sports. Get up a group and play volleyball, soccer, baseball, basketball—whatever you know how to do that gives you a good workout.

▽ Play individual sports. Tennis, gymnastics, and fencing are all great exercise that you do alone or with another person. Or try rock climbing or hiking.

▽ Hang glide or sky dive. This is very exciting if you have the nerve. People who do it claim that once you try it, you can become addicted.

▽ Ride horses. Take lessons if you've always wanted to learn. Even in large cities, there are parks with stables where instructors hold classes.

▽ Dance. This is wonderful aerobic exercise. You

can learn to touch dance with a friend. Do jazz or tap dancing. Try Greek folk dancing or English morris dancing. Go back to your own roots. If you can't find a class that interests you, hire an instructor and set up your own group.

You can think up hundreds of more ideas. Results, however, will be found not in the thinking, but in the doing. Just get started at *something*. Set small goals, and keep a record of your progress. It's very gratifying to note even a little progress from one week to the next. To succeed, you must make a commitment of time and attention. We're always having to rearrange priorities. If health and fitness have not headed your list up to now, you might want to rethink your priorities. Your reward will be peak vitality—the energy to help you attack your life plan with enthusiasm and confidence.

8

YOU'RE ON DISPLAY

"You never have a second chance to make a first impression!" is the slogan of experts whose job it is to see that women go out into the world looking their absolute best.

There's a lot that goes into looking your best. In the previous chapter, we discussed the basics—what you need to do before you even start to think about clothes, and makeup, and all the other individual touches that make your style your own. You should have a firm body, and a glow of good health, and an aura of vitality. Energy attracts people. And a great-looking presentation—your wardrobe, accessories, hairstyle—is the icing on the cake.

Looking good is important to anyone who goes out in public. And that includes just about everyone. Whether you are visiting relatives, applying for a job, running for local political office, or even shopping, you have to pay attention to your appearance. Why? Because it's going to make a difference. It makes a difference in how you feel and what you project.

It's human nature to gravitate toward those who project self-confidence, who seem in control of their situation. The way you tell the world that you're all of those things is to start with yourself. If you look well put together, with a little pizzazz that's the result of having your own style and feeling comfortable with it, your audience knows that:

▽ You pay attention to detail. You make a plan and carry it out. You don't let things just happen. You're in control.

▽ You have pride and self-confidence. You have chosen to look a particular way. You are not hiding behind monochromatic, baggy clothes of no discernible style.

▽ You care enough about yourself to make a statement. This gives you personality. Will everyone think that statement is terrific? Not necessarily. It doesn't matter. You must have confidence in your own judgment.

What You Wear

The details of the clothing that you choose to buy are completely up to you. There is only one rule: dress should be appropriate for the occasion.

"Appropriate" means:

▽ Elegant enough so that others look at you with pleasure.

▽ Conservative enough so that you don't ruffle old-fashioned feathers.

▽ Distinctive enough so that you look like you and not everyone else at the party or meeting.

▽ Comfortable enough so that you can put on the outfit and forget about it.

ARE YOU A PACK RAT?

A pack rat is a rodent that hoards all sorts of unnecessary objects. Sound familiar? What do the closets and drawers in which you keep your wardrobe look like? Perhaps it's time to:

▽ Look at every single item. If you haven't worn something in a year or more, be ruthless. Give it away, unless it's a priceless Southwest silver concho belt that you think your daughter will like someday.

▽ Review what's left with a friend. Friends are very important in the whole area of personal appearance. You really do sometimes need another opinion—and someone to see how an outfit looks from the back. A friend will tell you to get rid of something that you were ambivalent about. A friend will tell you that you look just great, which is nice for your self-esteem.

▽ Organize. Show off your ability to create order. You ought to know just where every element in your wardrobe is. And you ought to be able to get together a suitable outfit for *any* occasion in just a few minutes.

That means you have to *have* the correct clothes. Be sure that you own: both a casual and a dressy sports outfit, a conservative go-to-business dress or suit, and something drop-dead for evenings out. You don't need more than one emergency outfit in each category, but it should be complete. You should have bag, shoes, accessories, all clean and polished and ready to go.

Every article of clothing that you own has a:

▽ Style
▽ Fabric
▽ Color

It is the choices that you make in each of these categories that determine your final look.

Style. This is the cut of the sweater, coat, dress . . . whatever else you need. The style of an article also determines where it fits into your life. Is it dressy? Good for a picnic? A day at the office?

Someone once said that every woman feels most comfortable in the clothes she wore in high school. That may be true. But overcome that desire for Bermuda shorts and knee socks or wheat jeans and sweatshirts or torn clothes with decorative safety pins. You're an adult now.

What is appropriate for a grown-up woman to wear?

▽ Clothing that you like. You want to express your own personality. Apparel is too expensive for you to waste your money on something that you don't really respond to. You should feel as if you've acquired a new friend.
▽ Clothing that is classic in style. By "classic" we

mean styles that have proved favorites for years—that are flattering, and comfortable, and fun to wear.

Many working women went astray for a few years when they tried to simplify their wardrobes by copying their male co-workers. The result was lots of women in every sort of job wearing gray-flannel suits—sometimes *three-piece*—with oxford-cloth shirts and floppy bow ties.

Not everyone felt very comfortable with this style. This rigidity in the dress code has given way to greater flexibility and freedom as women have gained more confidence at work.

Women don't need to dress like men in a work environment because they're *not* men. In our culture, there are really only a few acceptable ways for a man to dress. But a woman has many choices—suits, dresses, pants outfits, high heels, low heels, different hairstyles and makeup. A clever woman can change her look almost totally by twisting her hair up in a French knot and putting on full evening makeup. The most a man can do is dress in evening clothes.

In a work environment, you have the same large choice that you would have in choosing a dress for a wedding. You would pay some attention to the sort of environment you're in. If you're in a business situation, and not working for yourself, take a look at the women on the management level above you. They're probably good examples of what's accepted in your office.

You could wear a suit, but you would choose something with some personality to it. An interesting jacket, for example, without lapels, or with oversized buttons. A dress with a jacket is also a good choice.

Keep to a style that you're comfortable with, and like, and soon people will perceive you as having your own "look." Thumb through the fashion magazines, and see what's available in the stores—knowledge of what's out there is important if you're going to be a good shopper. But don't slavishly follow fashion. Usually the people who look best in extreme fashions are the designers' models, and sometimes even they look a little silly.

Here's where your friends or in-store fashion consultants come in. Discuss with them what looks best on you and try to stick to those styles. Certainly, you will try to accentuate your good points (wear belts if you have a narrow waist) and camouflage those that are not so good (avoid cap-sleeve blouses if your upper arms are not firm).

There is great diversity in skirt lengths these days—from mini to mid-calf. Just don't be too extreme. In general, skirt lengths are best just above the knee. But there are lots of exceptions. You can certainly go shorter if:

—You're young at heart and have great legs.

—You're in the fashion industry and are expected to look up-to-date.

—You live or work in a milieu that is very fashion-conscious and super-aware of changing styles. In situations like this, if you're too conservative, you're going to be conspicuous and out of place. It would be better to find your own style within the avant-garde framework and go with it.

Middle-aged or elderly women should not wear their skirts too short, but at or just above the knee is just fine. As we go into the 1990s, women in even our most conservative cities are wearing their skirts shorter.

▽ Clothing that may be a little different can also be appropriate. You might really enjoy wearing slacks, even in a work setting. It may be that most of the women—and all of the women executives—wear dresses or suits to the office. That doesn't mean that you can't *occasionally* wear a pants outfit to the office. This will not be jeans and a sweatshirt, but a really smart combination—perhaps dressy slacks with a silk blouse and an interestingly cut jacket.

▽ Clothing should be well made. Is there enough material in the seams? Do the seams pucker? Is the item lined? Are the buttonholes hand-sewn? Are buttons of natural materials (bone, pearl, or wood)? Is the fabric of good quality?

You will find your clothing budget better spent if you go for quality and simplicity.

Clothing prices differ depending on where you live, but say that you spend $200 for a dress with a jacket. Are you going to get your money's worth? Let's assume that you've chosen a basic style, one that you can wear practically anywhere.

A good dress will clean properly, and not shrink a size or two every time. And the fabric should not stretch—it will hold its shape and look fresh and new for a long time. You will probably get more than twenty wearings out of your expensive dress.

If you choose a basic style of whatever the item, in a fabric that is not too busy, then you can change its look by the addition of a scarf or a belt buckle or a cardigan sweater. You don't necessarily want everyone to remember that long orange skirt if you've worn it to the office party three years in a row. A long black or red lamb's wool skirt would have been a better choice. You could have worn different tops and jewelry on the separate occasions and no one would have noticed the skirt was the same—just part of another handsome outfit.

Fabric. The same rule applies to fabric as to the workmanship of an article of clothing. It should be of good quality.

Clothing made of synthetic fabric doesn't wrinkle—but stains can be hard to get out, and the colors are often harsh and too vibrant.

Natural fabrics are the most attractive but wrinkle badly. Think of a 100 percent linen skirt after you've sat down in it once. But many clothes are manufactured today of wool, cotton, or linen with just a little bit of synthetic added to retard wrinkles. These are usually a good choice.

Another excellent choice: any of the lightweight

wools or jersey knits. Clothing made of these fabrics can be worn comfortably all year round. They're perfect for traveling because the clothes hold their line and don't wrinkle very much.

Color. You can wear any colors that you think are flattering to you. These are usually colors that harmonize with your skin tones. Your skin might be light or dark, but it will have either yellow/peach undertones (the warm colors) or pink/blue undertones (the cool colors). Just remember: the more yellow in a color, the warmer it is. The more blue, the cooler the color.

Any woman can wear any colors at any time. And they can be warm colors *or* cool colors. But do coordinate the various colors of a particular outfit, and be sure that the colors you've chosen harmonize with your makeup as well—warm with warm, cool with cool.

What are your best colors? Some women are more knowledgeable about colors than others. You may have a very good idea about the underlying colors that make up your skin tones, and know your color wheel, and which colors traditionally complement each other.

But if you don't, there's a foolproof way to discover which are your best colors. When do you get compliments? When you wear deep blue? That's a good guideline. Pay attention the next time someone tells you that they like what you're wearing or says that you look terrific, and did you lose weight? It may be nothing more than a pretty mauve sweater that brings out the best of your hair and skin tones.

Don't feel stifled and think that you have to wear the same colors over and over. Experiment. Some outfits will be more successful than others, but we're a long way from the days when a redhead wouldn't even consider wearing pink.

Don't forget black—it isn't called "basic" black for nothing. Black is the one color that can go absolutely anywhere, anytime. You could have nothing but black in your wardrobe and still appear perfectly dressed at all times.

But at the least, every woman ought to have two black dresses—one for day, one for evening. The daytime dress could be a simple knit—the perfect thing to dress up or down. You could wear it to the office, and then out to dinner. The dress for evening would also be of simple cut, but perhaps of a dressier fabric—something that you could feel comfortable in at cocktails or a black tie dinner.

A black—or navy—suit is absolutely essential if you work, or go out a lot, or have meetings of any sort. It's the perfect item to dress up or down—and you're always appropriately dressed.

Keep in mind that your body is not necessarily like your best friend's. Camouflage the faults, highlight the good points.

Tall and thin? No vertical stripes. Short and stocky? No horizontal stripes. The idea is that you don't want to accentuate a physical feature that's too much of anything: tall, short, fat, thin.

Do you wear hats? They can sometimes add drama to an otherwise rather uninteresting look. Pay attention to the shape of your face. If you have a small, heart-shaped face, don't hide it. Wear a small hat on top of your head. Do you have a long face? Top it off with a hat with a wide brim. Don't *emphasize* the lines of your face; wear hats that offer contrasting angles.

If you like hats, be sure that they're appropriate for the time and place. Hats *are* fashionable again, but only in certain environments. They are hardly ever suitable in a place of business. Do a little research before you put one on. Make sure that it will add to your outfit, not make you look a little odd and out of place.

Is your complexion sallow? You can improve a sallow complexion by wearing rosy colors. You will benefit from the glow. And once you've decided what colors are best for you, try to keep your purchases within the broad range of coordinated shades. Then you'll be able to mix and match outfits more easily.

Once you've gotten it all together and have a clear idea of the sort of clothing that is flattering to you, think about how you *wear* your clothes. An otherwise impressive effect will be wasted if you let your clothes dominate you. You have to stand and sit so that you appear enthusiastic and ready to meet the world. If you slump, and peer out from between hunched shoulders, you will not give the self-confident impression that you're trying for.

Most of us had posture training in grade school. Remember how we were taught to stand up straight? Let your arms and shoulders hang naturally while you imagine a string attached to the center of your head going straight up to the sky. Your spine and head are kept in a straight line by that string, when you're sitting or standing. You shouldn't become frozen in an unnatural attempt at "good posture," but relaxed and able to move freely. You will breathe more easily, which is both energizing and relaxing. You get energy because more oxygen is filtering into the bloodstream, and relax because deep breathing causes a lot of tensions to disappear.

Your Accessories

Accessories are all those things that go with your basic outfits: bags, shoes, hats, belts, scarves, gloves, jewelry. These are the items that:

▽ Actually *do* dress an outfit up or down. Example: you're going to dinner directly from work. You wear your basic black knit dress. Your jewelry for the day is plastic—fun geometric earrings with colored plastic bangles. For evening, you tuck a silk scarf into the neckline of the dress and change to gold earrings and bracelet.

▽ Change the look of your basic wardrobe. Accessories don't only dress up or down—they make something different. Try a red bag and shoes instead of black with your taupe knit dress, or a man's sleeveless argyle-patterned wool vest over the gray sweater and skirt that you've worn fifty times.

▽ Are fun. You wouldn't want to be *too* amusing by buying an expensive cashmere sweater with a very unusual pattern—better to stick to basics there.

But why not experiment with a new scarf? Toss a scarf over your shoulder or drape loosely around your neck. There are a number of ways to wear scarves, whether they're oblong or square. Many manufacturers include booklets with their products that contain scarf-tying ideas, and there are even entire videos devoted to this invaluable accessory.

▽ Can help you extend the life of an article that has seen better days. Do you have silk slacks that are perfect in every way except for the indelible stain at the waist? Buy a man's wide cummerbund in a color that goes with the slacks and your troubles are over.

YOUR LEATHER ACCESSORIES

Accessories that are made of leather—your belts and shoes, for example—should be of as good a quality as you can afford.

They will:

▽ Last longer. Cheap leather creases and cracks almost immediately.

▽ Stay fresh. Leather breathes. You want your belts to look just-bought for as long as possible. A belt that's scratched and creased will add exactly nothing to your outfit.

▽ Be more comfortable. Many women find a shoe manufacturer whose styles they like and whose shoes *fit*. You can't think about anything else during the day if your feet hurt. You're on your feet for a large part of each day. An investment in a comfortable, and elegant, pair of shoes is money well spent.

YOUR MOST PERSONAL ACCESSORY: JEWELRY

There was a time when most people wore only real jewelry, and silver and gold chains, bracelets, earrings, rings were the way to go. Sometimes it looked great, sometimes boring, but it was rarely a great addition to the *costume*. And hardly ever did it absolutely make the outfit.

Then designers of all sorts got into the act, and jewelry became central to the completion of a chic effect—fashion jewelry was born. In addition to precious metals and gemstones (which will remain forever important as articles of adornment), jewelry was now made of every sort of material: plastic, aluminum, wood, paper, pottery, gold- or silver-toned metals, painted metals, stainless steel, iron, found objects . . .

And the shapes! Jewelry can now be found large, small, very large, in forms that look as if they were made by a sculptor, which indeed in some cases they are. You can find interesting jewelry everywhere from Tiffany's to the "everything under $5" shops on a highway. Never has there been such a good opportunity to express your own personality. Also, much of it is inexpensive, so you can indulge different moods. There is still a place for your grandmother's cameo, but now every woman can have a complete wardrobe of jewelry. And new pieces are a terrific way to update some outfits that are looking a little tired.

Here are a few tips so that your fashion jewelry always looks bright and new.

ᐁ Maintain luster by buffing each piece occasionally with a soft, dry cloth.

ᐁ If you wash your jewelry, rinse thoroughly and pat completely dry.

ᐁ Always remove fashion jewelry before sports, swimming in salt water, and showering.

ᐁ To prevent discoloration, avoid exposing jewelry to perfumes, hair sprays, skin cream, and salt water.

ᐁ Store pieces carefully, so they won't rub against each other.

ᐁ In order to preserve the finish, store jewelry away from cosmetics. It should also be kept in a dry area—too much dampness will ruin most finishes.

FYI—A Glossary of Fashion Jewelry Terms

Gold electroplate: An 18-karat gold coating, heavier than goldtone finish.

Gold-filled: An actual layer of 14-karat gold permanently bonded to base metal.

Goldtone: An 18-karat gold coating of goldwash or goldflash over base metal.

Silverplate: A base metal coated with silver by an electroplating process.

Silvertone: A coating that has the look of silver (but doesn't necessarily contain silver) over base metal.

Sterling silver: The finest quality. It should be at least 92.5 percent pure silver.

Rhodium: A metal of the platinum group, frequently used to plate silverware to prevent tarnish.

Carat: Unit of weight for diamonds and other gems.

Karat: Unit of weight to express the proportion of gold in an alloy.

Lengths of necklaces:

Choker—15 inches.

Princess—18 inches.

Matinee—20 to 24 inches.

Opera—28 to 30 inches.

Rope or lariat—40 to 45 inches.

Cabochon: An unfaceted cut stone of domed form.

Faceted: A type of cut gem bounded by plane faces.

Baguette: A style of cutting small, rectangular gemstones, principally diamonds, into a rod shape.

Cloisonné: A type of enameling in which various colors of enamel are separated by thin wire bands that are first soldered on a base to form a design.

Pavé: Many stones set flush with the surface to show the least amount of metal.

Peridot: A mineral species that yields yellowish-green gemstones.

Rhinestone: Colorless imitation stone of high luster made of glass, paste, or gem quartz.

Cultured pearl: A pearl produced by artificially inducing the formation of a pearl sac into the body mass of a pearl-bearing mollusk.

Mother-of-pearl: The iridescent lining of the shell of any pearl-bearing mollusk.

Simulated stone: Any substance fashioned as a gemstone that imitates it in appearance.

How Do You Wear Jewelry?

There *are* a few guidelines. There are four basic places available for a woman to wear jewelry. (We're not going to discuss the fingers because many women wear the same rings all the time.)

1. Wrist.
2. Ears.
3. Lapel.
4. Throat.

You would not want to wear jewelry on all four spots at one time. It's fashion overkill, and very confusing. The eye doesn't know where to look first. But there are interesting combinations that do make design sense:

∇ Earrings, a pin, and a bracelet.
∇ Necklace, earrings, and a very small pin.
∇ Remember that a prominent belt buckle must be considered a piece of jewelry: thus, a large gold buckle, a gold bracelet, and a smart pair of earrings would really be enough for daytime wear.

The style of jewelry that you buy would depend not only on what you liked but also on what sort of person you are physically.

The same rules apply that you follow when choosing hats.

∇ If your face is square, with straight, angular lines, then wear rounded pieces of jewelry to offset the sharp features.

▽ If your face is round, angular or geometric pieces will cause the viewer's eye to move vertically. Pieces that add length, like dangling earrings, are a good choice.

▽ An oblong, or rectangular, face needs width: choose short necklaces to reduce the length of the face, and don't wear drop earrings.

▽ If your face is heart-shaped, or triangular, and tapers to a narrow chin, wear earrings that are wider at the bottom than the top. Also, choker necklaces to soften your pointy chin. Avoid necklaces that come to a V—they give un-needed accent.

What Color Is Best for You?

You should think not only of the shape of your jewelry, but also its color. What would look best on you?

Your skin is:

▽ Olive, darker tones: Bronze jewelry is great.
▽ Sallow, pale: Red is an energizer.
▽ Tan: White.
▽ Cool skin tones: Silver, platinum, white gold, dark gemstones.
▽ Warm skin tones: Gold, bronze, copper, light gemstones.

Your hair is:

▽ Brunette: For jewelry, silver, pearls, burgundy, garnet are all effective.

▽ Gray: Silver and platinum.
▽ Auburn: Gold, amber, tiger's eye.
▽ Blond: Gold, coral, pearls.

Your eyes are:

▽ Blue: Try the colors found in sapphires, aquamarine, lapis.
▽ Green: Emerald, hazel tones, jade.
▽ Brown: Topaz, amber, tiger's eye, amethyst.

Your Look

Although it's fun to get it all together and appear to the world just as you'd like to be seen, it's also serious business. People make quick judgments when they meet you, and it's both good business and a boost to your psyche when you get a favorable reaction.

You don't have to be a fashion victim and follow all the latest trends blindly. But do be aware of what's current. Then it's up to you whether you accept or discard an idea. Taking control of your appearance means that *you* make the choices, and adapt styles to fit your taste and needs.

The way you look is one area of your life that's constantly changing—and improving. And it's an area in which you can dynamically express your personality. The look that makes you feel on top of the world and able to do anything is within your power to create.

9

COMPLETING THE IMAGE: YOUR HAIR . . . SKIN . . . FACE

Sometimes when children ask their parents for a dog, the response is no, because "Who do you think is going to end up taking care of it?" This is a realistic answer—after all, dogs have to be walked every day, no matter what.

Something similar can be said of hair and skin care, as well as makeup application, because you have to deal with these areas of your life every day, no matter what.

Many women, by the time they're adults, have worked out daily routines for hair and skin care. Nothing having to do with your general appearance is more important because this is the visible you, and you're showing it to the world every day.

The condition of your hair, and skin, and what you've done to your makeup mirror your health, and vitality, and your state of mind. Is your hair glossy and healthy? Do you have a good haircut? What about your face? Do you look rested? Do you look attractive?

What's inside is bound to show on the outside. You want to show that you're happy, healthy, and in control. And nothing shows that control more than the appearance you present to friends and strangers alike: attractive, complete, and exhibiting the image that you've decided on for yourself.

Do *you* have a routine that you're comfortable with for hair and skin care? Do you know what makeup you should buy and how to put it on? If you don't, read on. You, too, need a daily routine that you can live with.

Hair Care

You should think twice before doing *anything* to your hair.

A bad haircut by a helpful friend can last for months. And you will feel anything but confident as you wait for it to grow out.

Loving hands at home should not apply to hair care unless you're *very* expert or have a friend who is a professional. Lacking that, you should consult with your hairstylist—and keep trying until you find one who suits you—about everything having to do with care, cut, color, styling.

The danger areas for novices are:

▽ Home permanents.
▽ Coloring at home.
▽ Overcurling with a heated curling iron. Heat is just awful for otherwise healthy hair. Use your

hot rollers and curling irons for special styling needs only. Everyday use is too much.

And when you use blow dryers, towel-dry hair to cut down on blow-drying time. Always use them on low heat to avoid burning your hair and scalp.

Mistakes in any of these areas can lead to disasters that are not easily repaired.

You should leave the cutting of your hair to a professional. Discuss the style with this person, but don't bring in pictures of movie stars and say, "I want to look like her." You want to look like yourself. It's fun to change a style from time to time, but in general your cut should be suitable to the kind of life you lead, and you should feel comfortable with its length and shape.

During the 1960s, squared-off geometric haircuts were popular. Unfortunately, women without perfectly shaped heads and even features could not carry off the cut. But major hairstylists persisted in recommending this style, and many women walked around feeling quite self-conscious. Yes, they were "trendy," but the cut did not reflect their own personal style.

Be certain that your hairstylist is trying to please you, and will not use you as an experiment for some striking new hairdo ideas.

Your stylist should know you well enough to understand how you live. When you go to the hair salon, you're usually in a smock before you ever get to his or her station. The person who does your hair has no idea whether you spend your days in jeans and sneakers or knit dresses and high heels. Are you a working mom? A suburban housewife? A fast-tracker who has to travel a lot?

Your hair is part of your whole image, and the hairstylist will not have a clue what the right look is for you unless the two of you discuss it in depth.

A Rule of Thumb: For business purposes, it's safest to keep your hair shoulder length or shorter. If your hair is extremely long, and you love every strand, then pull it back or wear it in a classic chignon or French braid when you're in a work situation. Very long, straggly hair left over from your college days is not appropriate—it does not say "professional."

There are things that you could, and should, do at home.

BRUSHING YOUR HAIR

Bend from your waist and brush from the scalp to the ends. Use long strokes. Don't use a harsh brush and don't scratch the scalp. Natural bristles are the best.

- ▽ The purpose of brushing is to lubricate the hair. Brush slowly so that you distribute the oils evenly along the hair shaft from the root to the end. Rapid brushing doesn't help at all and may split ends.
- ▽ If your hair is fine, use softer bristles; if it's coarse and curly, stronger bristles. The bristles should have rounded tips.
- ▽ Keep your brushes absolutely clean. Wash in a basin with warm water and a little shampoo. Dip and swirl around. Don't soak because prolonged immersion will loosen the bristles.

Don't wet the back of a wooden brush. Rinse in lukewarm water and wipe the handle dry. Shake the brush to get rid of excess water. Put the brush, bristles up, on a towel and let dry naturally.

▽ You can forget those one hundred strokes a day. In these days of frequent shampooing, it's unnecessary. The original point was to remove dirt and keep the hair as clean as possible. Twenty strokes daily is plenty to remove loose hairs and surface dirt.

▽ Do you use hairspray? Brush it out every night. Too much spray can make the hair brittle.

▽ Never brush wet or damp hair. Wet hair is very elastic, and too much pulling can cause stretching and breaking.

SHAMPOOING YOUR HAIR

However often you wash your hair, the result should be that it's always squeaky clean.

If you wash frequently, every day, for example, don't worry. You won't dry out your hair. Only soap once and use a gentle shampoo. You'll have to experiment until you find the right shampoo—they come in countless different formulations. You may find after prolonged use your hair doesn't respond the way it did. Give your hair a rest and try a different brand.

In general, if your hair is:

Dry. Wash gently every other day. Follow with a soft rinse-out conditioner.

Normal. Wash thoroughly every other day. Use a cream rinse.

211 ❧

Oily. Wash well every day. When ends feel dry, condition.

Damaged or tinted. Wash according to hair type. Use a deep-penetrating conditioner once every two weeks to restore moisture.

When shampooing:

1. Brush your hair first. This will distribute oil throughout the hair and loosen dead cells.

2. A shower is the easiest way to wash your hair yourself. Use warm water and wet hair thoroughly.

3. Don't pour shampoo directly on head. Put a small amount in your palms first and rub together to build up a lather. Comb your fingers through your hair to distribute shampoo evenly. Massage your scalp gently with your fingers, *not* your nails. Work suds from scalp to the ends of the hair and massage lather into your hairline.

4. Rinse well with lukewarm water.

5. Unless hair is very dirty, you don't need to shampoo twice. Rinsing is fine, though—run as much water through your hair as you like.

Hair care experts say that you should spend four times as long rinsing as in shampooing.

6. As soon as your hair is absolutely shampoo-free, use a conditioner. Some are formulated to be left in the hair and some to be rinsed out after a few minutes. Read the instructions carefully.

If your hair has been damaged by outdoor exposure, or too many chemical treatments, you may need a conditioner that will help repair it. If you don't know what to use, consult your hairstylist.

STYLING YOUR HAIR

With the help of your hairstylist, you can learn to maintain your look during appointments. Your haircut should be good enough so that your hair keeps its line until it's time for a trim.

If you have a hairstyle that needs help to stay in place, learn to use the various styling products on the market.

Gel. Use on wet or dry hair. Will mold and help hold a style and increase shine. Gives a "wet" look.

Mousse. Use on wet or dry hair. Also holds style. You can reactivate mousse by misting hair with water and rearranging.

Setting lotion. Helps hold style. Work into the roots to give lift and volume to your hairstyle.

Hairspray and styling mist. Holds style. Can be used to help you style while blow-drying.

Your Nails

When you meet someone for the first time, you make eye contact and give them a firm handshake. Their first impression of you is going to include whether you have a firm gaze, and what condition your hands—and nails—are in.

You could splurge and have a manicure and pedicure at a professional salon, but if you'd rather spend the money on a really good haircut, you could certainly take care of your nails yourself, following a few simple steps.

There are lots of products easily available for nail

care. At the least, you need: an orange stick, emery board and nail file, nail clipper, cuticle pusher, nail brush, and buffer. Whatever you do, never, ever use a metal implement. It will cut and tear your cuticles and defeat the purpose of a manicure. Wood is the material of choice.

You can buy nail enamel in any colors that you like. But buy colors that will harmonize with your makeup. You might select a neutral or clear tone. They go with everything and tend not to show chipping.

YOUR MANICURE

Step 1. Remove the old polish. Do it with a cotton ball soaked in nail enamel remover. Hold cotton ball down on nail for a count of four, then slide it toward the tip.

Step 2. Shape nails. Use an emery board or file. Hold it horizontally and file to the nail tip, following natural line of your cuticle.

Step 3. Moisturize cuticles. Let softener absorb for a minute or two.

Step 4. Push back and trim cuticles. Use your cuticle pusher. Start in the middle and move up one side and back. Repeat on other side. Apply cuticle remover and trim ragged spots.

Step 5. Mend any imperfections and smooth ridges with your buffer.

Step 6. Brush on base coat. You might start with a strengthener and then follow with a clear base coat.

Step 7. Brush on nail enamel. Begin with the little finger. Let enamel dry for two minutes. Then apply second coat.

Step 8. Apply top coat.

Your Feet

You need to pamper your feet. We've all experienced the agony of having to get through a day trying not to think about a big toe squashed into a shoe that was uncomfortable.

When your feet are tired, you're tired. When your feet hurt, you can't think about anything else very clearly.

How do you put your best foot forward?

1. Exercise. You want to relax your feet, and you want to strengthen the muscles.

Try a free-form exercise that will do both: you just have to walk barefoot for fifteen minutes a day.

Do you ever go to the beach? Walk barefoot in the sand. Not only does it strengthen foot muscles, but it will slough off calluses as well.

2. Alternate heel heights. Don't wear the same-height heel every day. If you change off, the muscles of your feet and legs will be well toned.

3. When you're tired, remember those poor feet. You will feel much better if you soak your feet, and let them enjoy a pedicure and some foot sprays and talcs to keep them comfortable and dry.

YOUR PEDICURE

Step 1. Remove polish with a cotton ball saturated with nail enamel remover. Clean nail surface and beneath tip with cotton-wrapped orange stick dipped in remover.

Step 2. Smooth and soothe feet. Soak feet to soften

cuticles. Soak in warm water and moisturizing foot soak for ten minutes. Pat dry with towel. Apply sloughing cream to rough areas and calluses. Gently massage with foot brush.

Step 3. Trim, file, and shape toenails. If you use a nail clipper, cut off only about one-sixteenth of an inch at a time. Use a coarse-textured emery board for shaping.

Step 4. Apply cuticle softener. Leave on for a couple of minutes, then massage. Push cuticles back with your wooden cuticle pusher. To trim ragged cuticles, apply cuticle remover and snip off with special cuticle scissors.

Step 5. Moisturize and massage with cream. Clean toenail surfaces with cotton and orange stick to remove excess cream.

Step 6. Improve imperfections by buffing and brushing on problem-solving solution. Follow with clear base coat. Let dry for two minutes.

Step 7. Apply nail enamel. Match enamel on fingernails. Let dry two minutes. Apply second coat.

Step 8. Apply top coat.

Your Fragrance

The world of fragrance, which includes perfume, cologne, eau de toilette, scented creams, gels, and bath oils, is fun and filled with the opportunity for experimentation.

You can pick and choose among the many products available to you, governed only by your own sense of smell. You can find floral scents, woodsy blends, spicy, fruity fragrances, and some fragrances that seem steeped in the mysterious aromas of the Orient.

If you've always worn the same fragrance, it's time to experiment with at least one new one. If you wear the fragrance year-round, try changing your fragrance as the seasons change. It's a terrific way to give yourself a lift.

Start by testing a fragrance on yourself to see if you like it. Remember that what smells good on your friend will not necessarily be the same on you. Each person's body chemistry is different and affects the fragrance scent. Here are a few tips to keep in mind when you're testing fragrances: try no more than three at a time—use your right wrist, left wrist, and lower arm. More than three fragrances will start confusing your sense of smell. Let the fragrance dry for about ten minutes—that's when you'll experience its true essence on you.

Layering is a popular way to have fun with your fragrance. By using different forms of the same scent, you can intensify it and benefit from all-over body fragrance. Try a scented soap, bath foam, or gel in the bath or shower. Follow with a body splash. Moisturize with a body lotion or perfumed skin softener. Pat on a perfumed talc or velvety dusting powder. Finish with a spray of cologne on your pulse points (wherever you feel a heartbeat).

At the same time, be careful how much fragrance you put on in the early morning—you may get to the office to find yourself absolutely reeking of your favorite scent.

Whether the fragrance you wear is decided by your mood, the season, what you have on, or all three, the important factor is that you are wearing it. It always makes you feel better—more in control!

Your Skin

Your skin is the mirror of your general health and frame of mind, and there is no other part of your body that requires more attention or care.

What you put into your body shows up eventually on the surface of your skin. If your diet is good, with plenty of fruits and vegetables and lots of cleansing water to drink, your skin will get the nourishment it needs.

If you drink and smoke, it's going to cause problems eventually.

We've all seen the ruddy complexion and broken blood vessels of the heavy drinker. To say nothing of puffy skin folds around the eyes. Obviously, too much alcohol is bad for you in a hundred ways, and will affect all your body systems.

A few words about smoking: it's hard to be ambivalent about smoking as it's just plain bad for you.

It's lethal when it comes to your general health. There are thousands of articles and books available that talk of heart problems, and lung cancer, and strokes, and emphysema, and decreased circulation, and involvement with the pancreas and other organs. And asthma, and bronchitis, and ulcers, and headaches. Those who can stop should, right now; those who can't should try professional help. Millions *have* stopped. You just need to find the right motivation.

In addition to all the other horrendous damage smoking can cause, it's terrible for the skin. Because smoking causes breakdown of the collagen that holds the skin together, smokers wrinkle much more than nonsmokers. And heavy smoking contracts the blood supply to the skin, which affects healing. Some plastic surgeons won't operate at all on heavy smokers.

Because smoking seriously depletes the oxygen supply in your body, your skin is not nourished properly and will wrinkle much more easily.

Smoking can cause social as well as physical problems. Recent statutes in several states have banned smoking in many places where the public congregates.

And what about a work situation? The basic rule, which is only common sense, is DON'T LIGHT UP! It's very unprofessional.

If you're in a room with people whom you've worked with for ten years, and they all smoke, and you're working together on a project, then it's probably okay for you to smoke, too. But if you're in any but the most familiar old-shoe business situations, no cigarettes.

In general, you're never too young to start skin care—and you're never too old. Nothing ages a woman more than neglected skin. Most women don't have to spend a great deal of money on skin care each year—one estimate talks about less than $100—but they do have to pay attention from the time they're old enough to think about how they look.

Are you starting a new business? Then you're under a lot of stress. That stress is going to show on your face, and if you want to continue to look your best, you're going to have to double your efforts to counteract the effects of strain and fatigue.

Some do's for skin care . . .

▽ Use a sunscreen daily. And use a more potent sunblock, with a higher number, every time you're going to be directly exposed to the sun. The number that you use depends on the shade of your skin and also how easily you tan or burn. These days, many kinds of cosmetics, like foundations and moisturizers, come equipped with sunscreen.

▽ Learn to wash your face properly. Treat it carefully, and don't scrub. Use gentle cleansing products.

▽ Use the skin care products that are easily available. You don't have to go overboard, but the minimum should include a cleanser and a moisturizer. If you have the time, you might want to consider "specialized" products: products that address a particular concern you have—wrinkles around the eyes, enlarged pores, or simply aging skin. Try using a once-a-week mask to deep-clean. Night cream for delicate areas gives protection while you sleep.

▽ Remember that the condition of your skin changes. This depends on the time of year, the time of month, the climate that you live in, and your age and general health. Choose products that are formulated for the condition of your skin *now*. You may have to change products several times a year.

▽ See a dermatologist if you have a problem with spots, or acne, or discoloration.

▽ And the most important do: never skip daily skin care. Get into the habit of a regular routine. Use your cleanser, and toners, and moisturizers. When you use these products, remember your neck. It's part of your face and you should think of it as such. Start at your neck with any of these skin-care products and massage upward, using small, circular motions to get into the pores of the skin.

Keep in mind that prevention is basic to good skin care. What you do to prevent aging, wrinkling, discoloration, damage of all kinds, is much more important than what you have to do later to conceal the flaws.
Some don'ts . . .

▽ In the cold weather, don't go out without a moisturizer.
▽ Don't overdo sun exposure. It's just awful for your skin: it dries, ages, wrinkles, destroys. It's certain that there is a link between the sun and skin cancer later in life. Why risk it?
▽ When you're in the sun, don't ever use a sun reflector or metallic reflector blanket. Serious burns might result.
▽ Never experiment with anything harsh by yourself—like a chemical peel. Leave it in the hands of the experts.
▽ Never go to sleep with your makeup on. Go to the trouble of removing it properly and let your skin *breathe*.

Your Makeup

Makeup is an enhancer—not a mask. You use it to conceal blemishes, tone down features that are not your best, highlight those that are. You can learn to become a great painter, and your face is your canvas.

There are many ways to learn how to use makeup effectively:

▽ You may have a friend who has been creating miracles with makeup ever since she was a little girl. Have a session with her.

▽ You may know an actor. He or she will know everything about possibilities. While you don't want a theatrical-makeup look, the techniques of enhancement and concealment they're familiar with will be useful.

▽ Department stores often have experts at work at the cosmetics counter. Of course, they want to sell you their products. Keep in mind that you're not obligated to buy anything that you don't need, especially if it's more than you want or are able to spend.

American women have begun to realize that they don't have to pay $20 for a lipstick. When you buy the upscale lines, you're buying prestige—which not everyone cares about—a product, and some very expensive packaging. Women are beginning to rebel at sky-high cosmetics prices as they use the more moderately priced products and find them just as good.

▽ Beauty salons often have consultants, and even

your hairstylist might have an interesting opinion. Any of these people could take a look at the shape of your face and your skin tone and give advice.

∇ There are books, magazine articles, and videotapes that will tell you everything you need to know about making up from crack of dawn to late nights on the town. Buy one and experiment with a friend.

The wonderful thing about experimenting with makeup is that if you have a disaster, just wash your face and start over.

Although you don't need every product on the market for good makeup results, you do need a few basic products. Your makeup wardrobe should include:

1. Foundation. It may include a sunscreen. It will even out your complexion, hide blemishes, give your face some color. Furnish yourself with a nice canvas on which to paint the other colors.

When buying foundation, select a shade that goes with your skin. Test it along your jawline. If it blends with the color of your neck, that's the shade that's right for you.

Obviously, don't ever apply it to your neck, but stop at the jawline with a feathering, blending motion, so that it doesn't look like a mask. Use your fingertips or a sponge to apply. Contrary to skin-care products, foundation is applied from the top of your face down, with the grain of the skin. Use a down-and-out motion for a smooth application.

2. A concealer product. For dark circles under the eyes, age spots, any imperfections.

Select a color that's one shade lighter than your skin tone. You don't want to look like a raccoon, so blend the concealer in very well.

3. A blush. It can be a cream, or powder, or come in pencil form. You want to give your face some color. It should look natural, not painted on. The idea behind rouge or blusher is that it's a natural color of your skin—a healthy blush.

To find the natural placement for your blush, just smile. The color should start at the apple of the cheeks and then be blended along the cheekbone, stopping before the hairline. This method works quite well with about 90 percent of all women.

Add a little blush across your forehead and a dot on the chin to balance the color.

4. An eye product or two. Mascara is used by most women. Make sure you change it every few months if it's not used up, as bacteria can form, leading to eye infection. Mascara makes the eyes look larger.

Select black mascara unless you have extremely fair eyelashes and hair, in which case you would use a dark brown.

5. Also try eye shadow or pencil. This could be a fairly deep shade—something in the brown family, or plum, or smoky gray—to really outline the eyes, to give them some emphasis. You will look less tired if you really define the shape of the eye.

Keep the color smudged close to the eyelashes. If you use more than one color, then put the darker color on the outer corner of the upper lid. If you use color underneath the lower lashes, just carry it about a third of the way along the lower lid, not to the inner corner.

About glasses. The glasses of those women who are near-sighted tend to make the eyes look larger, so you can wear a little less eye makeup. If you're far-sighted, your eyes look smaller, so wear a little bit more.

6. Lip color. It could be lipstick, a gloss, a pencil. This is for accent, to finish off the picture.

Lips are very vulnerable to sun damage. Lip color products now contain sunscreen for protection and will also prevent drying.

Remember your color coordination. Cool colors have blue/violet undertones, warm colors have yellow and orange—the fire colors. Your dress and makeup colors should be chosen to coordinate with each other—and keep your skin tone in mind when selecting your colors.

What If You're a Mother-to-Be?

Some of you are, or will be, pregnant, and you have special needs. During pregnancy, an inner radiance shines through—something perhaps that nature has built in to compensate for a less-than-graceful figure. Whether you feel you have been endowed with this glow or not, you need to be more aware of grooming at this time and may need to make temporary alterations in your usual beauty routine. A few points to keep in mind:

▽ Change in hormonal balance can affect the complexion. Overactive glands leave some women with acne; others say their skin has never been so clear.

▽ Your skin may be drier than usual. Pay special attention to moisturizers.

▽ If you have facial blemishes, or change in skin pigment, try a sheer liquid foundation to even out skin tone.

▽ Brownish stains can develop on the forehead, cheeks, or nose. These are called the "mask of pregnancy." It's mostly found on brunettes, and, although there is no way to prevent it, it does disappear after the baby is born. You can camouflage these marks with a cream or stick concealer in a shade lighter than your own.

▽ Sometimes increased blood circulation causes too rosy a skin color. Soften with powder and avoid pink-toned foundations or blush colors.

▽ If your skin is pale and drab, brighten it up with light, soft tones of blush—powder or cream.

▽ Eyes can become a focal point by wearing neutral eye shadow shades and a thin, smudged line of pencil. Avoid heavy eye makeup under the eyes: this will accentuate any darkness or circles under the eyes.

The Final Product

Your final look is the result of a lot of thought, and hard work, and smart shopping, and exercise, and creativity.

In almost no other area of your life do you have as much control as you do when you decide how you're going to appear to others, and how you're going to feel inside.

It's never too late to:

▽ Improve your health.
▽ Improve your fitness.
▽ Improve your wardrobe.
▽ Improve your knowledge about skin and hair care.
▽ Improve your expertise with makeup. Feeling tired? Makeup can conceal. Feeling depressed? You can improve the way you look so dramatically that the clever use of makeup can lift your spirits.

When you look good and feel good, this is translated into a kind of self-confidence that is attractive to others, and gratifying to yourself. The bottom line: you have succeeded in doing wonderful things with yourself. You can do wonderful things in the world outside.

EPILOGUE

ॐ

"The gods help those who help themselves," said the storyteller Aesop in the days of the ancient Greeks.

All the Women of Enterprise winners would agree with this idea, as would any woman who knows what it is to have a dream and try to make it come true. To overcome, to succeed, you must nurture traits that each of you possesses.

These traits—passion, determination, self-confidence, and pride—underlie all your successes. They are part of your character and personality. But sometimes they become rusty through disuse and you have to bring them to life to make them work for you. Some of our Women of Enterprise winners show how this is done.

Passion

Heida L. Thurlow, a 1987 winner with a passion for gourmet cooking, has translated that interest into a multi-million-dollar housewares business.

Thurlow, who earned a degree in mechanical engineering from West Germany's Essen Institute, wanted to start her own business so she could more easily combine work and family responsibilities. Using her technical know-how, Heida Thurlow designed a line of elegant oven-to-table cookware, and Lentrade, Inc., of Houston, Texas, was launched.

Excellent, innovative products were not enough. Thurlow found, like many other women entrepreneurs, that money was not readily available. Says Thurlow, "Only when I found a bank with a female VP did I get a loan for my business without my husband's guarantee." Coco Chanel, the great dress designer, is her role model because "Chanel was the first woman to fight her way into the men's designing world."

Heida Thurlow believes that your passion can be translated into a better way of life. She says, "Through my children, I have met many homemakers who would love the challenge of creating their own business. Often they underestimate their capabilities and I would welcome the opportunity to encourage them to believe in themselves. Most mature women have had to develop excellent organizational talents and the capacity to improvise. If they would apply these talents toward building unique businesses, it would not only give them greater fulfillment, but it would also give us, the consumer, a great wealth of wonderful products and services."

Determination

"Determination and a great desire for success" underlie Mary G. Winston's drive to better her family's condition. When asked to identify the single most important quality she possesses that has helped to lead to entrepreneurial success, she says, "Perseverance. I am a firm believer in setting goals and working hard to achieve those goals. I've had my share of obstacles and stumbling blocks, but I keep trying to do the best that I can."

What appear to be obstacles and stumbling blocks to Mary Winston would be insurmountable barriers to someone else. This 1988 Women of Enterprise Awards winner is now the president of Winston Janitorial Service, in Indianapolis, Indiana, a company with annual billings of more than $3 million that employs 270.

There is nothing in Winston's background except patience and the will to succeed that would predict this sort of success.

Mary Winston was the daughter of an Alabama sharecropper and the oldest in a large family. Only eleven when her mother died, Winston had to leave school to care for her younger siblings. But she was determined to get an education any way she could: for her, it was correspondence courses.

By 1953, Winston was married and working hard. She had a full-time job supervising the cleaning force at a U.S. army base and, to supplement their income, she and her husband began cleaning private houses, sometimes working until 2:30 in the morning.

The next step for the Winstons was full-time attention to their own business—which gradually shifted to commercial cleaning. The business grew slowly but steadily, with both husband and wife working together, until 1977, when John Winston died.

For two years, Mary Winston floundered. Should

she sell the business or try to continue on her own? Her competition in Indianapolis predicted failure, but Winston was determined to prove them wrong. Winston Janitorial Service went from success to success, and in 1979 she landed her first large government cleaning contract. "It's not easy," says Winston, "as a woman to go in and pick up government contracts. You have to have a reputation."

Winston's reputation rests on first-rate service and dependability. Today, not only does she head the largest woman-run janitorial service in her state, but she also serves as an inspiration for black youth from poor backgrounds. Says Winston, "I've always wanted to be a living example and a role model for our young generation. I have decided that when I leave this world, people will know that I've done some good and made a difference in someone's life."

Self-confidence

May Yue, a 1987 Women of Enterprise Awards winner, has that sense of self-worth that is characteristic of so many of our winners. Says Yue, "True success is to achieve true happiness. True happiness is knowing that you love yourself and others and that whatever you do, you feel worthwhile."

Yue learned to be self-confident as she built success on success over the years.

When she was four, she and her family fled from Communist China to Hong Kong, where they remained until she was a teenager. Next stop, the United States, with its economic possibilities. May Yue completed college with a degree in home economics, and after some work experience in both Hong Kong and the United States, she decided that her true interest lay in the field of financial planning. Getting training at a financial planning firm, Yue bypassed upper-income clients to concentrate on the middle classes.

They could benefit enormously from financial planning, thought Yue, and in 1979 she brought her ideas to life and opened her own offices, Financial Services Associates, of Edina, Minnesota.

Her sales seminars to reach potential clients were very successful, and Yue could put her theories to work. More important than financial rewards for herself, though, is the "tremendous sense of well-being knowing that I have made a lot of money for my clients, many of whom have limited means. I feel that I have helped them fulfill their dreams."

Pride

Juliet C. Welker, a 1989 Women of Enterprise Awards winner, is today president of Welker Real Estate, in Philadelphia, Pennsylvania. What makes this entrepreneurial venture unusual is that Welker is a black woman who has managed to become an important business force in what was Philadelphia's predominantly white Museum of Art area.

Welker was brought up to be proud of her heritage and was taught that success was within her grasp. She remembers her Great-aunt Willa, who said to her,

"Never hold a negative thought. Always think positively. Have faith in your ability to succeed and have faith that God is on your side."

Juliet Welker approached the job market in 1973 well prepared, she thought. She had a master's degree in city planning from the University of Pennsylvania and was ready to work.

First stop—she applied for a job with a real estate company that promised "training—no license or experience necessary." But when Welker applied, the requirements suddenly changed and she was told to return after she'd earned her real estate license.

Welker—frustrated but not to be stopped—did just that. This time the Realtor agreed to hire her, but she could sell only her own listings. She tried other real estate firms, but no one would take a chance on a black salesperson.

Juliet Welker was not going to give in. She took the job with its conditions and tackled the difficult job of selling real estate in a white neighborhood.

She learned her business, acquired a reputation for quality and good service, and in 1977 opened her own office. Times were rocky at first, but Welker, who had little management training, hired a consultant to hone her skills.

Welker heeded her Great-aunt Willa and continued to think positively. Her business prospered, eventually topping annual sales of $12 million.

Juliet Welker quotes Martin Luther King, Jr., and continues to hope that black people "be judged not by the color of our skin, but by the content of our character." She is proud that she could "play a small role in helping make this equality a reality. . . . My acceptance is far from 100 percent and I must daily overcome racial barriers. However, the fact that I run the leading real estate office makes the statement that the community has chosen excellence of service over racial bigotry. I feel very proud to have made this happen."

What Does This Mean for You?

It's within your power to change your life—as soon as you decide you *want* to. Your life is yours to control, no one else's.

Our Women of Enterprise winners all had one thing in common—they refused to accept their limitations. With courage and conviction they found ways to challenge the limitations, to overcome them, to take control, and make far better lives for themselves and their families. They accepted the fact that their lives were their own to design.

Now it's your turn. If you answered the questionnaires in this book and found you were not totally in control of your life, or if you've been aware that your life is somewhat out of control, start making changes today. Start slowly. Make one or two small changes at a time. Prove to yourself that you possess the power to alter your life positively. It will give you the confidence to take bigger steps in the months ahead.

And if you decide to be a woman of enterprise, don't be surprised if you suddenly feel very uneasy. Probably every woman who is running her own business today felt just like you when she first started out—apprehensive, afraid to take the risk, wondering if she really had what it takes. Remember, you're not alone. Millions of women who are running their own businesses are there to support you, to encourage you, to help you begin and to help you grow. All across the country, the U.S. Small Business Administration offices and women's business groups are waiting to provide you with information and support.

As we've said throughout this book, you deserve to have the best life possible. It's within your power to have it. We shared with you the "secrets" of our Women of Enterprise winners. As you think back now on what you've read, was there anything really secret about what they did? We think you'll agree there wasn't. Their "secrets" are nothing more . . . or less . . . than these four qualities of the spirit:

Passion . . .

Determination . . .

Self-confidence . . .

Pride . . .

You need almost nothing else in life. If you have these traits in abundance, and can learn to use them, you will be able to set a goal and reach it.

The Women of Enterprise Award winners are ordinary women who have accomplished extraordinary things. When they set out to reach their goals, they didn't know what the results would be. But they did know they wanted a change, to make their lives better for themselves and their families, and they knew it had to be within their power. We know the same will be true for you.

ABOUT THE AUTHORS
ề

Gail Blanke capably juggles multiple roles as wife, mother, business executive, and motivational speaker. Avon's vice president of public affairs is the quintessential contemporary American career woman. Blanke has spearheaded a series of corporate programs designed to support women's financial independence. She is a graduate of Sweet Briar College in Virginia and attended Yale University Graduate School of Drama.

As Avon's national beauty and fashion director, Kathleen Walas travels nationwide each year to give interviews for network television, radio, magazines, and newspapers. Millions of women benefit from the beauty and self-development advice she provides. Wife, mother, experienced entrepreneur, and co-owner of a thriving beauty care business, Walas formerly served as a consultant to such celebrities as Mary Tyler Moore, Kim Alexis, and Dorothy Hamill.

Additional copies of *Taking Control of Your Life: The Secrets of Successful Enterprising Women* can be ordered by sending a check for $17.95 (please add the following for postage and handling: $1.50 for the first copy, $.50 for each added copy) to:

MasterMedia Limited
215 Park Avenue South
Suite 1601
New York, NY 10003
(212) 260–5600

Gail Blanke and Kathleen Walas are available for speeches and workshops. Please contact MasterMedia's Speakers' Bureau for availability and fee arrangements. Call Tony Colao at (201) 359-1612.

OTHER MASTERMEDIA BOOKS

THE PREGNANCY AND MOTHERHOOD DIARY: Planning the First Year of Your Second Career, by Susan Schiffer Stautberg, is the first and only undated appointment diary that shows how to manage pregnancy and career. ($12.95 spiralbound)

CITIES OF OPPORTUNITY: Finding the Best Place to Work, Live and Prosper in the 1990's and Beyond, by Dr. John Tepper Marlin, explores the job and living options for the next decade and into the next century. This consumer guide and handbook, written by one of the world's experts on cities, selects and features forty-six American cities and metropolitan areas. ($24.95 cloth, $13.95 paper)

THE DOLLARS AND SENSE OF DIVORCE: The Financial Guide for Women, by Judith Briles, is the first book to combine practical tips on overcoming the legal hurdles and planning finances before, during, and after divorce. ($10.95 paper)

OUT THE ORGANIZATION: How Fast Could You Find a New Job?, by Madeleine and Robert Swain, is written for millions of Americans whose jobs are no longer safe, whose companies are not loyal, and who face futures of uncertainty. It gives advice on finding a new job or starting your own business. ($17.95 cloth, $11.95 paper)

AGING PARENTS AND YOU: A Complete Handbook to Help You Help Your Elders Maintain a Healthy, Productive and Independent Life, by Eugenia Anderson-Ellis and Marsha Dryan, is a complete guide to providing care to aging relatives. It gives practical advice and resources to the adults who are helping their elders lead productive and independent lives. ($9.95 paper)

CRITICISM IN YOUR LIFE: How to Give It, How to Take It, How to Make It Work for You, by Dr. Deborah Bright, offers practical advice, in an upbeat, readable, and realistic fashion, for turning criticism into control. Charts and diagrams guide the reader into managing criticism from bosses, spouses, children, friends, neighbors, and in-laws. ($17.95 cloth, $9.95 paper)

BEYOND SUCCESS: How Volunteer Service Can Help You Begin Making a Life Instead of Just a Living, by John F. Raynolds III and Eleanor Raynolds, C.B.E., is a unique how-to book targeted to business and professional people considering volunteer work, senior citizens who wish to fill leisure time meaningfully, and students trying out various career options. The book is filled with interviews with celebrities, CEOs, and average citizens who talk about the benefits of service work. ($19.95 cloth, $9.95 paper)

MANAGING IT ALL: Time-Saving Ideas for Career, Family, Relationships and Self, by Beverly Benz Treuille and Susan Schiffer Stautberg, is written for women who are juggling careers and families. Over two hundred career women (ranging from a TV anchorwoman to an investment banker) were interviewed. The book contains many humorous anecdotes on saving time and improving the quality of life for self and family. ($9.95 paper)

REAL LIFE 101: (Almost) Surviving Your First Year Out of College, by Susan Kleinman, supplies welcome advice to those facing "real life" for the first time, focusing on work, money, health, and how to deal with freedom and responsibility. ($9.95 paper)

YOUR HEALTHY BODY, YOUR HEALTHY LIFE: How to Take Control of Your Medical Destiny, by Donald B. Louria, M.D., provides precise advice and strategies that will help you to live a long and healthy life. Learn also about nutrition, exercise, vitamins, and medication, as well as how to control risk factors for major diseases. ($12.95 paper)

THE CONFIDENCE FACTOR: How Self-Esteem Can Change Your Life, by Judith Briles, is based on a nationwide survey of six thousand men and women. Briles explores why women so often feel a lack of self-confidence and have a poor opinion of themselves. She offers step-by-step advice on becoming the person you want to be. ($18.95 cloth)

THE SOLUTION TO POLLUTION: 101 Things You Can Do to Clean Up Your Environment, by Laurence Sombke, furnishes step-by-step techniques on how to conserve more energy, start a recycling center, choose biodegradable products, and how to proceed with individual environmental cleanup projects. ($7.95 paper)